The American Gentleman

A Contemporary Guide to Chivalry

Michael James Hall, MD

ISBN: 0-7596-7364-0 (E-book)
ISBN: 0-7596-7365-9 (Paperback)

This book is printed on acid free paper.

1stbooks rev. 07/16/02

CONTENTS

FOREWORD

You will not find a thousand-and-one "rules of etiquette" or a guide to hedonism in this book. Instead, you will find a gentleman's manifesto based on the life experiences and considerations of a young professional American man seeking social civility and greater personal character.

At the close of the twentieth century, some American men and women have devalued traditional values, like integrity and graciousness and other elements of civilized culture. Reflecting this mentality, our economy, popular media and entertainment have reinforced ideas and personal behaviors that are less honorable and less civil. Sadly, portrayed as a boor, the young American man is seen by some as self-centered and cowardly, behaving poorly and treating women disrespectfully. Yet, you may ask, why be a gentleman?

Simply, being a gentleman allows for character evolution. It confers to others that you are a man who actively pursues the moral high road and realizes your character, perpetually evolving, is linked to your deeds. Understand being a gentleman requires effort and self-sacrifice and a gentleman tries to give of himself without expectation. Equally as important, a gentleman is a man who respectfully places a woman's concerns before his own.

The American Gentleman strives to make life more fulfilling and is written to inspire men to adopt a personal philosophy for growth and maturity. Through observation, integrity, spiritual philanthropy, altruism and knowing reality is perception—a *state of character* can be formed for self-improvement.

Also, taking ideas from the past, the book offers some thoughts on courtship and rules of etiquette that have been updated for our modern life. To provide clarity relating to courtship and romance, the book offers chivalric principles as one way to develop mature and loving relationships.

Not dogmatic, *The American Gentleman* is written with certain questions in mind: How may "chivalry" be applied today? When does chivalry become chauvinism? Are there customs or behaviors that may improve personal relationships? How can men and women behave more harmoniously? In other words, is there civilized human behavior that can be identified, explained and formulated into a recognized standard and then applied to twenty-first century life.

The book is primarily intended to address the concerns of the modern American male through his character while maintaining sensitivity to the concerns of women.

In addition, the book briefly touches on our present social condition. As storm clouds gather on the horizon of American society, many men and women are seeking a greater meaning of life. Most troubling is the polarizing of American culture as divisive trends in political ideology, economics, sex relations and family dynamics are affecting the way Americans live. It is time for change.

The American Gentleman offers a path for men to achieve their personal goals while assisting others along the way. Enjoy.

Michael Hall, **MD** Manhattan, January 2001

PREFACE

Over several years, the idea of creating a simple book designed to inspire *chivalric* behavior among American men transformed itself into a complex manifesto of history, social commentary and personal theory.

Initially, I wanted to write a book defining the nuts and bolts of being a gentleman. What really appealed to me was not so much the mechanics of gentlemanly behavior or etiquette, but the collaborations of mind and matter that constructs a gentleman.

In pursuit of the gentleman's character, I sought not only the traditional, but a more contemporary and practical understanding. Once shrouded in romanticism, the gentleman has become a dying breed and is considered by some as an archaic, overtly paternalistic or even a chauvinistic stereotype. While maintaining the basic core of chivalry, *The American Gentleman* attempts to reintroduce the modern American man to aspects of virtue and tradition.

You might ask why can't men behave gentlemanly and also relate to the modern woman? Why do men have to stop being gentlemen? Can he continue living devoid chauvinism; can a gentleman exist without paternalism? Will he survive in the next century? I think that he can and I want to show you why.

The American Gentleman represents a shift to responsible and respectable male behavior. Men will behave and act chivalrously only if these behaviors and beliefs are taught. Because there appears to be little formal social training of gentlemanly behavior in American society, *The American Gentleman* offers social accountability and education, as well as an opportunity to reexamine what is acceptable behavior.

For example, as male attitudes toward women change, men are no longer perceiving women as vulnerable or less capable. Yet, frequently men behave indifferently toward women, unwilling to demonstrate common courtesy or respect. Perhaps some men are fearful that unsolicited courtesy will be viewed as sexism and rejected or more likely, they just don't know what to do. Does this concern you or someone you know?

Avoiding chauvinism, this book is designed for those who would like to understand and admire women for their innate differences. Quite honestly, *The American Gentleman* was written to celebrate women, to honor their unique abilities, and to appreciate them.

You may ask, why have we lost the gentleman? Let me try to offer my explanation. For millennia human life remained stable, predictable and change occurred in small increments. We also maintained well-formed social customs, courtesies and communities. National economies were based on providing sustenance and simple pleasures.

Today, due in part to technology, financial and social globalization, and unrestrained consumerism, customs and civility are practiced less abundantly. For instance, as our dependence on computers and instant information has become more essential for our lives, increasingly we are becoming detached from "flesh and blood" reality.

Also, with greater emphasis placed on workplace productiveness it's no secret the average person tends to work longer and socialize less. We all live in a state of constant motion with little time to reflect. Perhaps, we just do not have the time or patience to wake up, go to work, and be nice.

Today, extreme materialism and self-centered behavior violate the basic tenets of civil society. *The American Gentleman* attempts to point out the dangers of these behaviors to our public health. America should represent greater ideals. America is truly different from the rest of the world, in some respect it is an amalgam of the world, a land where people of different nationalities, religions and ethnicity can merge into one. We are a blessed nation.

Yet, ironically, the practices of American democracy, liberty, and capitalism may be partially responsible for the scarcity of national civility and personal responsibility.

Why is chivalry important?

Quite simply, one day our children will have children, and it is the responsibility of all Americans to ensure their innocence is protected. *Being a gentleman* offers men an opportunity to conscientiously manifest the necessary behavior to compel positive change to secure this goal. This ultimately requires men to take responsibility, be accountable and effectively lead their families and communities. What can you do to participate?

In my opinion, any one may become a gentleman by recognizing character evolution can only occur within an individual who manifests chivalric behavior and adapts a gentlemanly perspective. This is significant for three reasons:

- Accepting natural differences between men and women
- Promoting cultural tolerance
- Encouraging a more virtuous society

INTRODUCTION

During the final revision of the manuscript, it occurred to me that the reader would want to know why *I believe* I can write about being a gentleman. This is a serious question and one that is not easily answered. Therefore, I hope the following paragraphs will help.

When seeking a doctor, you primarily would want to know whether or not he or she has medical competence. To establish this, you might question where the doctor went to school, what sort of advanced training he or she has had, and whether their licenses, board certifications and hospital affiliations are in good standing.

It only stands to reason that without knowing much about the doctor's bedside manner or medical ability, their credentials provide at least the appearance of being whom they say they are. Yet, on the other hand, possessing the best credentials does not indicate how well he or she will understand your problem or be able to provide you compassionate treatment. Therefore, you have to use *instinct* and decide for yourself if the doctor is right for you.

My life story isn't much different from others who have wanted to become a healer, until I reached a momentous point in my professional life. I realized that the true mettle of a physician was tested when he or she provided more than empathy or care, but truth.

After realizing this, my medical career changed direction. I entered a unique field in which I had no previous experience, treatment of heroin addiction.

I soon observed, as heroin insidiously takes hold, life begins to unravel, drawing the user into an inescapable vortex of false illusions, feelings of invulnerability and joy.

The lure for many users is an imaginary, yet deceitful hope of creating a safer perception of life through a self-induced dissociation from reality.

Ironically, narcotic addiction offers a window into the very soul of man, revealing the primal urge to escape a cruel world and seek peaceful communion with all life. It is the combined force of physical need and euphoria that makes treating narcotic addiction so difficult. It is this reason why love, logic, jail and disease often fail to persuade many to change their behavior. To be fair, treating narcotic addiction requires slow and deliberate persuasion and a lifetime of therapy. This requires three important components: establishing social stability, creating new routines and introspection.

Stewarding the addict's recovery, I was permitted into the lives of my patients. I came to understand their problems, and they began to share their lives with me. With time I discovered their childhood, their families, and their dreams.

It is important to understand that the addicted are like anyone else, they are kind, bright and interesting people who want nothing more than to lead a happy life. Sadly, many use drugs to self-medicate past physical or emotional injuries in an effort to conceal their pain. I personally have come to believe that they cannot be faulted for their circumstances, as I am gradually understanding some of the reasons why a person might choose to escape, rather than confront reality.

So often, many people want to blame some genetic cataclysm or evil to explain why some people behave badly, abuse drugs and fail themselves and society. This usually isn't the case, as we are all born with abilities great and small and for us to understand, implement and enjoy them requires a caring family to foster confidence and instill discipline. Otherwise, they remain hidden and can benefit no one.

Incarceration, addiction, physical abuse, and other social ills including, to a great extent, incivility are all directly or indirectly caused by essentially one overwhelming circumstance—profound loss of unconditional love and guidance.

We are all products of both our environment and ancestry with little chance to change our personality or temperament, but it is my observation we can improve our character.

It is my professional opinion *character evolution* necessitates introspection and a philosophical change in thinking, as it is hard separating from the past. Yet, I know it is possible because I have seen it occur when my patients become drug-free and reclaim their dreams.

Even though the narcotic addict represents a social extreme, his or her story is representative of a larger society, an American society. Collectively, I believe America has forsaken its children, families and communities in search of a material high. We are creating a self-destructive society, as we have allowed our children's innocence to be harmed while many men and women seek to satisfy *themselves*.

Regardless, I propose to let you form your own interpretation of modern American society and permit me to discuss what I believe is required for the modern American man to become a gentleman, as the steps necessary for developing personal character and gentlemanly behavior really are not so different than defeating addiction. They require introspection, learning some new behaviors and living with grace.

So to answer the initial question regarding my qualifications to write this book, I can claim neither any special credentials nor can I say I am the ideal gentleman, as I know I have many imperfections. Yet, as you read the book I believe my ideas will provide you an accurate description of what I strive to be. As a doctor or a friend, I am the same person and I believe that like the gentleman, I am evolving while making a real effort to place the concerns of others before my own.

You may understand that the key to being a gentleman must involve:

- A willingness to evaluate your present behavior
- Honest consideration and appreciation of women
- Seeking fair and open communication with others
- Developing new social skills
- Living with grace

CHAPTER ONE

Chivalry, The Gentleman's Code, a Historical Perspective

"Without an adversary, prowess shrivels"

Seneca, *Moral Essays* Volume I

When you hear the term gentleman, what image comes to mind? If you are thinking of a well-dressed fellow with a penchant for custom-tailored shirts, welted calfskin shoes and a Montecristo cigar, you might really be thinking of someone else. These objects are only artifice for the true gentleman. Unfortunately, the "gentleman" today represents less chivalric ideal and more self-gratification.

What is the definition of a gentleman? If you look up *gentleman* in a dictionary, you will find a variety of definitions. As you read through them, you will notice that the word *chivalry* is used more than any other to define his behavior.

What exactly is meant by chivalry? Chivalry descended from the French root, *chevalier* or knight. Derived from the period of the Middle-Ages, the connotation could be considered the embodiment of idealistic values, beliefs, and behavior of this Renaissance warrior.

To begin understanding the concept of chivalry, it is important to understand civilization. Following man's establishment of complex society, two major forces have shaped all mortal communities and basic human behavior, wealth and war. Through worldly motivators such as greed and avarice, man has divided and labeled social groups of human beings into a variety of classes or caste systems. Class distinctions and

1

castes are common, and are seen in almost all human civilizations.

It was from the castes certain men were chosen and trained to perform social functions. The more intelligent, conquering or industrious participants were rewarded by their communities with privileges and from these groups emerged rulers, kings, and land owners, forming the top tier of the caste or upper class. It is this group that acquired most wealth through the labors of the majority. Others tacitly included in this class were those who help physically and spiritually heal, for instance priests and doctors.

Descending to the next tier, men of commerce or trade ran the economies of society. Established in the community, they made money for themselves and others as capital traders, merchants and by moving the materials and wealth of the first caste, land owners and rulers.

A third group was formed by those who comprise domestic functionaries, or bureaucrats who keep the society functioning properly. These people enforced the rules and governed the social order while ensuring their own existence.

The bottom tier, or servant class comprises people who usually are uneducated, subservient and destined to labor for the others. Perhaps imported or conquered, these people rarely could expect to become part of the other tiers.

Accordingly, there are several tiers of people in American society, roughly divided into three groupings: upper, middle and lower classes.

Although, America has a slightly atypical class structure compared to some other cultures, material possession is more meaningful than birth, education or cultural achievement and allows for class migration. As seen today, the nineteenth century French observer Alexis de Toqueville once noted Americans typically cycle wealth throughout the same family tree, as generations, one after the other, will often gain and then lose their wealth.

The knight could come from any caste, although he usually came from the first or second tier. He was a man guided by an ethos of cooperation and hard work. Likewise, over a period of several hundred years, European society produced a brand of formal behavior that defined what appropriate social conduct was for the warrior and builds the platform for chivalry. Flourishing during the Renaissance, chivalry established a philosophy for men, it formed a paradigm of personal, civil and moral responsibility that became a personal code of conduct. The knight was created, not born.

As a rule, it was through well established routines such as the patronizing of elders, professional and trade apprenticeships and the practice of "taking to arms" or warfare was a man to become a knight. Stoicism and mercy were idealized as essential traits while imparting their duties during warfare. A more modern example is exercised in American "Western" movies when a gunfighter establishes a tactical advantage over another, and allows the weaker party to survive. It can also be exemplified in the seafarer's phrase, "women and children first," as men were disciplined to think to protect the progeny, thus ensuring the survival of future generations by forsaking their own survival.

Men were also trained to reason and to pursue the art of brinkmanship to solve disputes, through the game chess or oratory exercises allowing him to practice the art of mediation, or diplomacy.

A good knight was political, adroit, observant and willing to care for his society, initially as a young warrior and possibly later as a magnanimous statesman. To act chivalrous was a function of having spiritual wealth and also could be considered as spiritual philanthropy. Unlike the religious possibility for forgiveness after repentance of sin, to act without graciousness was unforgivable.

Thus, a knight was a member of a select group of men distinguished by lifelong training in the service of the court and country. As roaming diplomats, they represented their king or queen and were expected to behave accordingly. Personified by their conspicuous social behavior, a knight embodied the enthusiasm of the Renaissance. It is important to keep in mind that their actions were conspicuous and not gratuitous. These were self-effacing men who typically did not usually expect reciprocity or recognition for their actions.

Critically, personal characteristics such as honesty, gallantry, fairness, kindness and generosity, especially demonstrated to the vulnerable and vanquished were very idealistic traits. Yet, why did they believe in this behavior? And how did they come to know it?

Let's look at a few questions and try to answer some basic points. First, was it necessary to be a certain personality type? Could their behavior be explained by their attitude toward life?

The argument could be made that yes, these men were not passive, *Type B* personalities, but they were aggressive, *Type A* characters. The knight is more like *Type A* in that they prided themselves in staying alert, carrying themselves successfully into battle and embracing challenges of long and arduous horse travel. They had to be confidently decisive, to take initiative and to be ready to react to any potential threat.

Second, what role did wealth or social status play? This is an interesting question. Stated before, wealth is not directly related to chivalrous behavior. Possibly, it is related to chivalrous behavior only in its ability to provide time to pursue endeavors like education. Being born wealthy was not necessary for a man to pursue an education and the training necessary for the rituals of the knight. Equally, there were plenty of men who were very wealthy and were considered nothing more than rogues. Education was considered important, as well as life experience and travel, as most knights were well seasoned with horse and ship voyages.

4

Third, did their lifestyle contribute to chivalry, or in other words, was there some component to being a knight that fostered chivalry? Owning a horse was a privilege, especially when this was the fastest type of transportation at the time. Also, these men were of a select group of men from different European cultures. Together, they would respectfully meet one another either as friend or foe throughout the European continent. In modern days, the legendary German Africa Korps General Rommel and his British counterpart, General Montgomery were the sort of men who deeply respected each other as accomplished warriors.

The fact that the knight traveled extensively among foreign cultures provided him a sense of understanding and appreciation of diverse human culture. They were able to accept differences more often than rejecting them.

Fourth, where did they learn chivalry? Who trained them? The training was well-defined, requiring education and instruction by both women and men at different times of their lives. As young men, the burgeoning knight was sent away to live with a woman, usually a woman other than his mother. The prospective knight was taught compassion, patient attentiveness and religious dogma by a pre-selected woman during his childhood. The period between his first and seventh year of life were devoted to establishing a moral foundation. He also was instructed on genteel behavior, manners, demeanor and the importance of character, as well as learning right from wrong.

After the age of seven the training shifted. He was then taught the skills in preparation for battle, riding and horsemanship, along with fencing and archery. Chosen, not unlike the career military officers of the armed forces of any modern state, the knight was entrusted to defend and to honor his respective kingdom. He also developed chivalrous behavior by imitating other men or role models, often these men were older, well-respected or admired in his circle of knights. Whether in battle or in society, the ideal knight conformed to a higher standard.

For instance, caring for the weak and invalid, showing mercy toward a vanquished foe, and humbleness are important Christian traits. As seen with the Arthurian knight, displaying courage or performing great deeds with an unusual sense of self-effacing disinterest and aloof consideration was the essence of grace.

With reference to women, the ideal knight displayed as unquestionable respect and appreciation for women. Women were considered to have special significance, and this distinction directly related to their childbearing abilities. At this time, science was not capable of explaining gestation. Therefore, a woman's childbearing abilities were considered by some as nothing less than miraculous.

In summary, although the European knight presented chivalric ideals long ago, there are archetypal characteristics that continue to parallel the gentleman of today. Throughout history, many authors, scholars, and historians have tried to define the qualities of the ideal men. A gentleman was described by the ancient Greek philosopher, Plato as the *guardian*, a virtuous man who, during his youth, defended the state and as an elder was chosen to become a statesman, a path not unlike some of our own American political leaders who are former war heroes.

The pursuit of gentlemanly behavior was not limited to Europe, for example, in ancient Eastern cultures such as India and China, great literary works like the *Kama Sutra*, circa 200 A.D., often considered by the West only as a sexual pleasure guide, was actually written by Indian nobility as a reference book for young men defining manners, grooming, personal conduct and the fine arts. *Kama* is Hindi and means, "sensual recognition of one's world combining the mind, body and soul." Designed to coach socially affluent men, it well describes the aspects of sensual appreciation as well. Furthermore, the Asian Indian subcontinent produced the Sikh warrior who like the

European knight demonstrated behavior considered chivalrous. There are many references to East Asian cultures, Japanese and Chinese in particular, that demonstrated chivalrous precepts as well.

To value the concept of chivalry, it is important to have an understanding of society and man. Reviewing history, we find that after man's establishment of complex society the two major forces that shaped all communities of men and women, as well as basic human behavior, are wealth and war. Class distinctions and castes are ubiquitous, and are seen in almost all of human civilizations and have given rise to the elements that form the early state warrior, or knight. Along with man's social order, there must be an attempt to strive toward an ideal. Chivalry is part of our past, and, if we choose, it will continue to be a part of our future.

CHAPTER TWO

The Early Gentleman

"The recognition in an enemy of the qualities one would wish to possess oneself, respect for a brave, able and scrupulous opponent and a desire to see him treated, when beaten, in a way one would have wished to be treated had he been the winner and oneself the loser"

Field Marshall Sir Claude J. E. Auchinleck, WWII

After the fall of the Roman Empire, circa 450 A.D., Western European creativity and inspiration was stymied for a period of some eight hundred years. This period, known as the Dark Ages, eventually gave birth to a time which reintroduced and reestablished appreciation of: literature, music, poetry, painting and the physical form.

After Europe's corporeal rebirth, men began to redevelop skills and trades, as well as building new centers of commerce and beautiful cities. Kingdoms were formed and reformed and so were the courts who ruled them. The geopolitical changes had an enormous impact on the education of men and as a direct result, the evolution of the gentleman.

Some men like the great French philosopher Rousseau had reservation and debated whether this period of *Enlightenment* was truly good for general society. Others contributed unique views of what this period represented. From the beginning, one individual who contributed to this debate and defined the qualities of the gentleman was Baldesar Castiglione.

Castiglione, a nobleman, born in the rolling Italian countryside of Umbria during the fifteenth century, had an enormous impact on the essence of the gentleman's perception.

As the Count of Novillara he made many observations and formed opinions through his personal interactions with noted scholars, poets, soldiers and courtly ladies. It was during a span of several evenings that he and his colleagues debated the essence of the ideal gentleman, which would later be refined for publishing and become *The Book of the Courtier*.

Ideals based on courage, elegance and wit were defined, explained and constructed into a variety of perspectives. The contributors were diverse, but were focused on determining what characteristics stood out among the gentleman. Finalized in 1528, the treatise embodied the essence of elegance and grace of a refined male character. Possessing intelligence, adroitness and civility, the courtier was admired and emulated by many. He was a role model.

The printing of *The Book of the Courtier* set a precedent among men of the time and quickly became a sought after manual and essential reading for would-be courtiers. As an authority on the gentleman, *The Book of the Courtier* made it possible for a man who has not been exposed to the social and personal elements of ideals and self-discipline to acquire insight and knowledge. It also demanded a transformation in collective social behavior.

In the late sixteenth century, the playwright William Shakespeare created many of his plays with *Renaissance* themes depicting some of his male characters as antagonists and protagonists who were struggling to distinguish themselves through virtuous character. Some of his most famous plays depicting the ideas of chivalry and character expressed during this time, which incidentally are still viewed today, were the *Taming of the Shrew* and *The Merchant of Venice*.

The eighteenth and nineteenth centuries are full of illustrations of men who tried to depict chivalric qualities that were eloquently defined by Castiglione. They were seen, more or less, in fashionable society of the growing cities of London, Paris, and Rome.

Similarly, modern American society has developed its own ideal male archetype, based on elements of courage, integrity and compassion. Due to the advent of the motion pictures, celebrated men of the silver screen era such as the Cary Grant, Clark Gable, James Stewart, and John Wayne became pop idols of chivalric character for millions of women and men.

Considered by many, as the gentlemen of America, they were admired and respected for their on screen performances that manifested gentlemanly character, charm and elegance.

Also, these men seemed to have had one thing in common, a fine appreciation of women, and an ability to listen with patient attentiveness. Classically, film stars who portrayed gentleman were not consummate unless they were able to intelligently penetrate a woman's mind. Demonstrating respect and deference toward the women they encountered, the gentleman usually offered gallantry in their exchange.

Gentlemen have usually distinguished themselves through their civilized treatment of women. Through principles of accommodation and deference, women were treated with great admiration and respect. Whether as the revered queen or the damsel-in-distress, women have, without exception, held a special place in the gentleman's heart.

A more modern example is illustrated with Ian Flemming's comical British sexist, *James Bond*, who through grace and courage saves the world, but still remains humorous and self-deprecating, and least not embraced by a woman.

Kind conduct expressed toward women has always been the mark of a gentleman, regardless of whom she is. This concept is paramount and essential for both understanding the ideal gentleman, and total self-fulfillment. A gentleman cherishes intelligent and kind women as integral to their personal and professional success.

As we embark the twenty-first century, the gentleman will continue to exist according to the times. Since the formation of society, men have established codes of conduct for many reasons. We will invariably continue to perform behavior that has social meaning, as demonstrated throughout most cultures. Valiant courage, respect, boldness, hospitality and integrity are characteristics that recur throughout the literature. While some of these behaviors are indicators of self-control, or a display of respect or deference, such as the act of holding a door for a woman, they provide social order. Therefore, it should be understood, the behavior itself is not so important, but the symbolism, as it serves to remind us that we are civilized human beings.

CHAPTER THREE

The American Man versus The American Gentleman

"Americans, while occasionally willing to be serfs, have always been obstinate about being peasantry"

F. Scott Fitzgerald, *The Great Gatsby*

The "American gentleman" is an oxymoron. It isn't because American gentlemen do not exist, it's just they really aren't a historical part of American culture. Unfortunately, the American gentleman is more an illusionary character as American society is saturated with examples of boorish male behavior.

Evidence of this observation was penned by the nineteenth-century English author and social critic, Fanny Trollope. During her travels throughout early America her stark portrayal of American life became the talk on two continents. She describes a telling example of American men:

"Gentlemen, in the old world sense of the term, are the same every where, and an American gentleman and his family know how to do the honours(sic) of their country to strangers of every nation, as well as any people of earth. But this class, though it decidedly exists, is a very small one, and cannot, in justice, be represented as affording a specimen of the whole."

Domestic Manners of Americans

This observation may be more or less accurate now as it was then. Today there are several stereotypes of boorish behavior among American men. There is the notorious *ugly American,* persona non-grata who is unwilling to adapt to foreign cultures and harshly demands the comforts of home while traveling abroad. This cliché represents pathologic individualism and self-centered behavior which violates the basic tenets of civil society.

The rural chauvinist, or *red neck*, is a person generally portrayed as uneducated and uncultured, often depicted as intolerant of others who are physically or culturally different. Another stereotype offered in American culture may be familiar as the malcontent notorious for arrogant and aggressive behavior, otherwise known as the *East coaster.*

These and other stereotypical personas are not limited by sex, race, religion, socioeconomics or education. Yet, why do these stereotypes exist? It should be said, stereotypes are not limited to our culture alone, as they exist in all cultures and in all nations to some extent.

As we focus on America, we must ask ourselves what makes us different from other cultures? Do we believe we are better than others? Is it fair to say arrogance or ignorance plays a role in these personifications?

There are several reasons that explain why American society is different from our European, African and Asian counterparts and why the gentlemanly persona is transparent in American society.

First, we do not and will not accept castes, class segregation or visible economic differences among ourselves. For example, we are fighting, and will continue to fight a class civil war in an attempt to balance perceived differences among American castes. It is clear, some Americans cannot accept others who have more material things or money than themselves. Irrespective of justice, Americans sue one another more than most cultures, with the majority seeking nothing more than quick monetary gain. Also, when Americans acquire wealth they often embrace the appearance of exclusivity and elitism. Pompous and ostentatious behavior demonstrates an insecurity with this newly acquired affluence. Briefly addressed in the previous chapter,

13

accordingly, a pecking order is quickly established based solely in raw material possession

Second, Americans deplore being ruled and typically scorn those in power. Remember that America was primarily settled by men and women who despised European aristocracy, and those associated with it. European immigrants migrated from their homeland to escape the monarchs, patricians and a social system that had curtailed their economic advancement and personal liberties, like religious worship. The American Revolutionary War was fought and won for these ideals.

Strong-willed, ambitious and described as "from the salt of the earth," many American settlers were not interested in carrying on the traditions of the European gentility. Idle, courtly behavior was held in contempt, and to this day many Americans still do. They were arriving in America to earn a living in professions as merchants, tradesmen and farmers. They were not interested in, nor had time to devote to courts, kings or chivalric ideals. Industrious, hard-working and tenacious are words that best describe these Americans, chivalrous behavior was limited to a very few.

As early Americans headed to a newly settled America, many sought to live life under God and establish a fairer nation. A majority of our predecessors held deeply devoted religious beliefs and believed in absolute freedoms prescribed by the Bible. They brought with them Judeo-Christian ethics and values that we still observe in present society. Some of these beliefs have come into conflict with others in our society who possess different and opposing beliefs. At times these conflicts have been contentious and have unearthed a divisive, if not destructive pattern of selfish behavior we see today.

Historically, early Americans were practical people and were building a new country. It isn't difficult to understand how formality may be compromised while populating the vast country side building homesteads, raising crops and fighting Indians. Common gentility was stymied by more earthly concerns and may explain why some American men fail to practice chivalric rite today.

During the Westward migration of settlers across the vast expanse of the American continent, hostile land was slowly tamed making way for hamlets, communities, towns and cities.

As these new communities flourished, their populace acquired social skills that became more sophisticated over time, albeit still below the average city-dwelling European. Some attempted to compare themselves with the European cultures of France, Germany and Italy in style but not substance. This is not to say European cultures were more honorable, as some exhibited great moral depravity and social abuse.

As mentioned previously, living in a society short on civility was well, American. It was not part of American social fabric to relate to the pageantry of the European gentility or take time to considerately reflect on the virtues of chivalry.

Yet, as a multifaceted culture, America does lay claim to its own nobility, unfortunately though, it is sheathed in the pains of human oppression. During the height of slavery, the South did produce, what has been described as Southern hospitality and the Southern gentleman. This man was considered courteous and well-mannered, perhaps even chivalrous and elegant.

As a Virginia plantation owner, it has been said that our own General George Washington sought social refinement as his memoirs noted two lessons he cherished from, oddly enough, an English magazine of civility: "Let your countenance be pleasant but in serious matters somewhat grave" and "Labor to keep alive in your breast that little spark of celestial fire called Conscience." Through inheritance, tariffs and land, these men were able to acquire wealth and status just as European nobility.

The plantation owners were similar to European feudal lords who used cheap labor to generate their wealth. But, it was a perverse form of feudalism because the laborers were not of this land, culture or religion, but snatched from a continent many thousands of miles away and forced into a hopeless existence.

Southern American nobility was similar to European nobility most likely because the men who settled the early South were from the courts of Europe and imported their pageantry, manners and customs while training their children the art of courtesy, horsemanship, and the use of a duel to defend honor. European culture and feudal economics were the driving force for evolution of Southern hospitality and charm. It is ironic that the same system that enslaved men, women and children could produce a gentleman.

Soon after destroying the native American Indians and occupying their land, American explorers found magnificent natural resources of gold, iron, wood and coal and soon their exploitation lead to a new era, the Industrial Revolution. This time of industry brought about tremendous financial speculation, new inventions and technologies, and a greater American presence in the world.

Wealth and prosperity became distributed among men who knew little about elegance and cared even less. They were entrepreneurs and speculators who began the great American tradition of, "striking it rich". These newly minted rich folks, or *Industrialists* were then catapulted into an old world, a world that had rules of etiquette and manners, a world where men and women behaved differently toward one another out of courtesy rather than necessity, a world where some men still inherited wealth and power, instead of earning it.

Virtually overnight some Americans became *faux-nobility*. Yet, as they acquired the material trappings wealth brings, they were still the hard-working, tenacious pioneers they were before, just with more money. The script of the ambitious American man or woman whose hard efforts eventually bear him or her wealth has become lore of any successful American business, and bringing folk hero status among their admirers to present day.

During the early and middle twentieth century, America was established as a world power. Americans engaged other nations in war. The Spanish-American War first asserted America as a super power, allowing it to brush off its backwoods, pioneer image and changing society's perception. Apart from a great loss of humanity, these wars also caused social and economic hardship and forced Americans, nationally, to come together for a common cause. For example, women entered the work force en mass, and for the first time, children were reared away from the home by surrogates.

World War II required great numbers of men who could literally kill, a strong military was formed, and instilled traditional chivalric values and battle hardened skills that shaped the American psyche.

Also defining global morality, World War II patriotically focused the nation toward traditional "American idealism". Americans fighting against Herohito and Hitler became a romantic fight between good and evil. After the war's end, the men who returned from these battles ushered in a profound respect for the importance of family, honor and tradition. Generals became presidents and leaders and role models were decorated veterans, there was a defined code of behavior for both men and woman. For example, men of the military lived by a code of conduct, many men who served their country with dignity, embodying the spirit of the gentleman after the war. This time was seen as simple and straight forward, and even by some historians and authors as the "golden age" of American life.

Not so dissimilar to the self-indulgence of ancient Rome or eighteenth century London, the late 1960's brought about a distinctly unique America. Shared behavior, considered by some as decadent and hedonistic, was different from past social expression as self-awareness liberated through sexual promiscuity and illicit drug use became "fashionable". Fueled by civil disobedience, apathy and a general loss of graciousness, the nation was propelled into a social and economic revolution against itself.

As a result, politeness and courtly behavior became less popular and were even considered by some groups as remnants of a bygone era with a perceived purpose to only confine and subjugate. To date, this *social war* has created significant misunderstanding as male and female relationships are now less certain and less defined.

As an illustration, men and women are in greater competition with one another now more than ever. One reason can be related to the acceptance of "wholesale feminism" which brought radical change into the personal lives and professional roles of not only women, but men as well.

Today, modern feminism has developed into a lobby and is a powerful political and economic instrument of the elite. It is my perspective that "feminism" was intended to expand the political, social and economic role of American women, without profoundly altering the special role women have with their children and family. By most standards, it has diminished the importance of American mothers and parents.

For instance, in modern society, men and women compete for the same incomes and status and both have chosen merciless strategies to advance their respective causes. Without question, this trend has had a negative impact on marriage, parenthood and child development, as well our American society.

The idea here is not to fault feminism, as Americans, we are all programmed from an early age to obtain personal material wealth and seek industrious lives. We are saturated with propaganda that heralds the doctrines of capitalism and our dependency on our consumer culture. Over time, old-fashioned street hucksters and snake oil salesman have evolved into ad agencies and television commercials suggesting a material reliance to be happy. Is it any wonder we compete the way we do?

In the new millennium, traditional values have a place and should be re-evaluated and reconsidered for life today. More relevant today, Americans seem willing to embrace what some may consider *Old World* ideals. The importance of tradition is applicable and worthy for our lives. For example, some young men and women are interested in assuming roles once thought of as gender specific. There is a resurgence of traditional values appearing in recent laws passed to encourage employment among welfare recipients and to discourage illegitimacy. Some women have left their professional careers to pursue family life while some young men are practicing abstinence until marriage.

It seems the pendulum of public opinion is swinging toward common sense to solve society's problems, and placing value on more defined and traditional roles for men and women. There are no easy answers, as it is difficult to understand our complex lives.

Regardless of the causes and reasons of incivility, realize that adapting a gentlemanly perspective is meaningful for three reasons: one, accepting innate differences between men and women two, promoting cultural tolerance and three, encouraging a more virtuous society. This is the quest of the American gentleman.

CHAPTER FOUR

Chivalry, Civility and the Individual

To act justly, to love mercy, and to walk humbly before
God

Micha 6:8, *Old Testament*

Chivalry and civility are inextricably linked. Civility is
defined as courtesy. Courtesy is defined as polite behavior
providing human beings a fair and honest way of interacting. It
is assumed that manners, etiquette, or whatever we like to call it
act as a social lubricant allowing people to peacefully coexist.

Yet, what has happened to civility in America? There is no
question civility has become less an importance as our lives have
become more complex. There is little debate that, the recent
social, economic and technologic advances have slowly removed
civility from our lives. Whether or not our ambition to conquer
the material world causes incivility is hard to prove, but it has
contributed to its decline.

As suggested in the introduction, one reason for the loss of
civil qualities can be related to the fact that today, there are fewer
mothers and fathers home to teach their offspring values and
manners. Parenting skills are no longer emphasized or practiced
as they once were due to: divorce, single-parent households and
illegitimacy. Today, economic concerns outweigh the
importance of ensuring children quality time with both parents.

For example, the number of children left alone at home after
school has created a new breed of child, or the *"latchkey kid."* It
is these children that rely on non-family members, mass media
and themselves to develop their behaviors, manners and values.
It isn't difficult to infer that the discipline necessary for value

formation or the mimicking of certain manners or etiquette is lacking. Let's look at the most powerful external force in the home, television.

As a highly influential tool, the television has replaced, for most families, other forms of learning or entertainment. Yet, it is reprehensible that most American children have been witness to tens of thousands of visually real homicides and rapes and thousands of separate violent actions. With no visible limit, raw violence and sexual crassness is seen in most programming at all hours of the day. What you may not know is a significant number of American pediatricians and numerous federal agencies, as well as, studies conducted by the Surgeon General have concluded that media violence has a direct negative impact on children and their behavior. Therefore, it affects all of us.

The evidence is undeniable and suggests the popular American culture we call "entertainment" is a significant threat to civility and a more important health concern than most people would like to admit. Conceivably, many parents are not willing to accept that they need to find alternatives to television to occupy their children's time. What values are needed for civil behavior? More specifically, how do we make certain we all get values that freely promote civilized behavior?

It is my opinion, of all the civil concerns presently, the most serious is the loss of the "traditional" family from American society. It is very important to have a strong familial presence to help train a young man to become a gentleman, it just can't happen without love and discipline.

If you assume most people are basically respectful and considerate of one another, then it also can be assumed that they would have learned these behaviors from observing others. And most would also agree, people who act disrespectfully and inconsiderately also learned these particular behaviors as well.

To illustrate this point, after John F. Kennedy, Jr. passed from the world in the late twentieth century, the loss of his short life was lamented not so much because of his name, wealth or physical prowess, but that he was a nice man.

Described by international nobility, the press and the man-on-the-street as considerate, thoughtful and decent, he was the embodiment of the American gentleman. Mr. Kennedy was indeed fitted with life's best material appointments, but it was his close bond to his mother and her strong desire to instill in him her values and sensitivities that made him a gentleman.

Many references indicate that the basis for determining the success of a child to be adequately educated depends almost entirely on the family. The role of a mother sets the tempo and tone of family life.

As mentioned before, the knight was well-educated by a female caretaker between the ages of one to seven, before he was to receive training in warfare or diplomacy. This period was considered the most important time for the formation of character and value building.

It has always been considered the root of chivalry for men to learn polite manners and etiquette from a respected female.

I believe, learning basic civil behavior from a respected woman is important or two reasons. Number one, the emotional bonds established during early life are important in developing strong self-confidence and high self-esteem. The nurturing bond between a mother and her son also promotes development of emotionally sensitive skills. For example, concepts such as sympathetic behaviors are experienced and learned because the brain is most receptive to conditioned learning between the ages of one to seven.

Therefore, if these skills are learned, they are remembered for life and become reflexive. In other words, they occur naturally and spontaneously.

Second, early pattering allows a man to interact with a woman without overt sexually driven motives. It allows a man to "do for" a female without the constraint of sexual favoritism. As an adult, with sexual desire, he is not compelled for a reciprocal favor for his kind act, (a kiss, a hug or anything else); he just behaves as he has been "naturally" taught.

Contemporarily, incivility has become an epidemic effecting both children and families and is showing no signs of slowing. Evidence of incivility between men and women is not isolated to the cities, but has become common to all regions and classes. For example, once termed as the "war between the sexes," incivility between men and women has become a major destructive force in our society, poisoning the very essence of our American culture.

The question that must be answered is, why do we need civility? Is there an advantage to being civilized? Some have described civility as the social grease that keeps harmony among men, and some feel civility will return, or we will not exist.

People throughout history have been held to rules. For example, Judeo-Christian teachings describe that from God, Moses handed man several thousand years ago the Ten Commandments. These rules still exist today and are considered essential for ensuring our civilization, as the court's sole function was to once offer judgment against those who violated these sacred tenets. Of course men and women break these rules and they often suffer consequences for their actions, yet it is up to the individual to behave correctly *by learning* acceptable social behavior.

Civility is no different, yet there are no written rules to follow and no one to punish you if you decide to ignore or contradict what is considered collectively good. There is no one to enforce good behavior, except perhaps parents.

For instance, if you allow a door to swing into another's face, you may receive a tongue lashing or a dirty look, but chances are you will not be punished. However, this is an action that most would consider discourteous and offensive. Incivility may occur anywhere, anytime. For example, the display of a cold glance after saying hello to a stranger, rudely stepping in front of someone in line or a lewd whistle toward a female passerby. As we know, these behaviors will not cause physical harm, but *psychologically* they might hurt. As well, these actions are not punishable by any law or court, and are therefore, grievances that we may choose to either ignore or collect and add to our daily anguish. Why is it necessary for incivility to exist? Do we really want to hurt others? Do we satisfy sadistic fantasies by these acts of omission or thoughtlessness? Is incivility an act of omission or a conscious action, a kind of payback for previous slights? Perhaps, we expect others to consider us, and then justify our incivility summed up by one female observer, "If they don't consider me, why should I consider them?"

It has to do with some of these reasons, but the more important reason is that, for the most part, American society doesn't expect us to be nice. Many have adopted an intellectual attitude best described as "why should I be any different from anyone else." This mentality rationalizes that we will not receive courtesy, and it presupposes incivility. This thinking becomes self-fulfilling, and many, therefore, refrain from being courteous.

We also live in a time when kindness is sometimes shunned. It may be that we have tried to help others in difficult situations only to find that our assistance is not desired.

In American culture there is also a sense of severe individual impartiality and a perpetuation of a legal belief, "no-duty-to-rescue rule" that continues to influence the way American society interacts. This idea relates to delinquent males injuring themselves and others and courts being reluctant to require another individual to help them upon request. There are many implications of this concept which are beyond the scope of the book, but suffice it to say that gender-correlated behavior is remarkably important in the eye of the court. Whatever the reason, civility to a large extent, is not being practiced in American society as much as some would like to see, and it has rippled into all aspects of American life.

The point is this. It is a difficult time for men and women. How do men and women show civility when American society doesn't reward its practice? How do men and women have time, with all that is required from them to earn a living, (new technologic challenges, working longer hours) or the will to practice civility? It would seem to make the practice of civility appear outdated and useless, especially when few expect civility to be practiced. Therefore, it is up to us to decide on our own behavior; we have a choice and we can choose to act with kindness toward others. And really, isn't that all that civility is, just kindness?

CHAPTER FIVE

Character Matters

"Truth does not become more true by virtue of the fact that the entire world agrees with it, nor less so even if the whole world disagrees with it"

Maimonides, *Moreh Novochim* 2:15

What is character anyway? Character is defined as a constellation of intellectual, emotional and moral qualities that distinguish one man from another. Character can also be a function of many components borne out of personal behavior, like integrity, altruism and spiritual philanthropy.

Character is independent of society. It is constant and resists moral relativism or the collective mentality for developing new definitions of virtues, mores and norms based on shifts in popular thinking.

For example, using illicit drugs is not safe. It is harmful to human physiological and psychological well-being, addictive, and has the potential to place you in a mind set and situations that may lead to more dangerous activities. Therefore, it is not healthy for an individual or society to "get high", regardless of its acceptance and usage in modern American popular culture.

Another illustration of this point is more pressing. In present American society, personal responsibility for one's actions appears forgotten. Men are following an extreme version of radical *individualism*.

Regrettably, many American men are running from the personal responsibilities they owe to their loved ones, their families and their communities. The logic behind this thinking requires only the justification needed to satisfy pleasure or desires simply based on will. More specifically, American behavior has become ostensibly more hedonistic, concerned only with satisfying our primal desires and indifferent to potential consequences. This thinking is flawed because it does not encourage men or women to consider the consequences produced by their behavior.

For instance, the 1960's sexual revolution has spurred behavior that is the hallmark of selfish thinking. The manifestation of HIV/AIDS, and other sexually transmitted diseases like gonorrhea, chlamydia, herpes and human papilloma virus are the direct consequences of ill-conceived sexual desire and participation. Ironically, as we become more educated and aware of the hazards, the less we are willing to amend our behavior.

Equally disturbing, American abortionists perform some 1.5 million abortions a year, with the majority overwhelmingly due to poor judgment and irresponsible behavior. The practice of abortion for many women is a form of birth control. There are other alternatives, yet as a society we choose to do what we want without consideration of the consequences to others. The previous statement is not to fault women for this trend but rather to indict men. Why should men be any less responsible? More importantly, we are a nation of citizens who lack the fundamental ability to take responsibility for our actions. Gentlemen have a duty to act responsibly and practice birth control also.

Nevertheless, since most of us like to attribute our failures to anything except our own shortcomings, it is natural enough for us to lie to ourselves and deny what we do. Very often, we do not admit when we are wrong. We attempt to persuade others through deceit, obfuscation or double-talk and often do not tell the truth. The evidence is all around us.

Recall the impeachment of the President of the United States during the close of the twentieth century. Inconceivably, a sitting President was found guilty of a degenerate pattern of behavior, perjury and obstruction of justice, in addition to lying to his wife and the country. Despite his personal life and media treatment, he had an obligation to uphold his sworn duty and failed to properly represent the American people. An American President is considered by many at home and around the world as the United State's supreme male representative and therefore, unquestionably held to a higher standard. As our country's military commander-in-chief, his personal judgment and integrity cannot be brought into question.

God and history will be the harshest judge of the former President, yet his legacy has negatively impacted generations of men.

It would seem that character no longer matters. It appears to been written off as an encumbrance for attaining power or financial and social rewards. Given the scandals and corruption of men in American politics, the failure of their moral and social leadership is an expectation. Today, we have become painfully aware only half of Americans vote and much less participate in demonstrations. Some have just given up or fallen down a slippery slope of cynical and apathetic thinking, "to expect and accept the worse." Yet, to sideline character and to forget its importance is wrong. Character does matter, there are people who live with it. So where are we to find praiseworthy character?

As an illustration, think about this question. How do people who do not understand a common language, or culture behave toward one another without fear or hate? Can there be some common element shared among people that is understood as benevolent and accepted as truth? Is it the same element that transforms an ordinary soldier, firefighter, or police officer to risk their lives for the needs of others? This is clearly demonstrated by the actions of the Good Samaritan who stops to help another after some terrible accident or tragedy. Perhaps, even on a smaller scale, this element is what defines a person who assists a frail person through a busy traffic intersection or holds a door open for a mother and her baby.

These are all examples of giving, giving of one's self. There is nothing expected, nor desired in return for these acts. They can be described as instinctive and finite. The reason for this most magnificent behavior is intangible and is part of our being, it is called altruism, also defined as compassion, kindness and love. You may be asking, how does any of this relate to the actions of a gentleman? It has everything to do with being a gentleman, a gentleman's philosophy centers on the generosity of his soul through his deeds.

Have you asked what makes a gentleman different from anyone else, "is there a universal pattern of behavior that might identify someone as a gentleman?" What word comes to mind that would describe what he has over others? I believe that grace best describes a gentleman's core. Grace is what separates the gentleman from other men. Different from religious *grace*, or Jesus Christ's salvation and forgiveness of sin, grace is a state of being, it is not a behavior practiced when a convenient opportunity arises. It is demonstrated without conscious effort and almost on an instinctual level and is performed without affectation. There is no appearance of trying. Grace comes from us naturally. It is useful to think of grace as art that does not appear to be art.

Can everyone have grace? Grace springs from the conscious heart. Not everyone has grace, but there are acquirable skills that can help develop it. What is required? There are no easy answers or slick rules to know. You do not need wealth or an education to have grace. What you need to start is willingness to see significance in others along with a consciousness. This concept will be discussed in detail later.

Can you be taught to see significance in others or inspire an awareness or consciousness? The truth is the way in which men and women relate to one another is due to many factors like: birth, parental guidance, social status, character, and temperament. Most of these elements are immune to change except for character. Our character is projected to the world based on our core values. These values are amendable and, if we choose, can resist conventional or popular influence. Through my professional experiences as an addictionist, I am certain character can be improved.

Character can be defined as moral or ethical strength. It reflects the emotional, intellectual and moral qualities of a person. Although it begins at home with our parents and develops throughout life, a gentleman must consciously work to shape his character through a conscious understanding of his priorities and beliefs while balanced between himself and his surroundings. Establishing a *state of character* is most important for being a gentleman.

This is achieved by developing a philosophy for living life completely, through interacting, sharing and experiencing all humanity has to offer within the context of good judgment. This is demonstrated by living without fear, ignorance and prejudice and by thoughtfully embracing each day and engaging new experiences. This requires risk or a form of "living dangerously" and works well to illustrate a part of this philosophy. Be aware, this is not to say a gentleman risks his life or others, or takes risk for the sake of proving himself. He risks by standing his ground, having courage and doing what he considers is right. A gentleman faces life as it is, learning to overcome obstacles through anticipation, preparedness, and action. The gentleman's philosophy is the catalyst for the development of his character.

CHAPTER SIX

The Gentleman's Character

"There is a destiny which makes us brothers no one goes his own way alone for what we send into the lives of others comes back into our own"

Anonymous

What ideas form a *state of character*? How does this philosophy build character? I believe it is accomplished through five key precepts. First, to understand and appreciate the world around you requires *observation*. To be aware of the needs and concerns of others, you must first recognize them. For example, as you exit a grocery line, you notice an elderly couple struggling with their bags in the check out line next to you. Instead of being impatient, you pause for a moment and notice that they are headed toward their car. It is this thoughtful observation that promotes your decision to ask if you may assist by carrying their bags. Regardless, if they accept your offer, the point is you made a respectful attempt to help. If you had not made yourself aware of their need, you would have walked past them and perhaps, their need for assistance. Observation requires that you see your surroundings and recognize you are not alone.

This idea is not new, and ancient mythology is full of fictional characters who through their actions have been used to teach us lessons. One mythical character, Narcissus, a male youth who obsessed with pride, lost awareness of his surroundings and was transformed into a flower, demonstrating the folly of self-obsession and vanity. The tip here is to see others and not only yourself.

31

You must make yourself aware of those around you, and then you will see that there are many people who could use a hand. Remember, a gentleman is aware of who he is, but he is not the focus. He also takes the initiative, is willing to lend a hand and is aware and never oblivious to the needs of others.

Second, gentlemen possess *spiritual philanthropy*. They give of themselves freely and expect nothing in return, expect perhaps a smile. It is as simple as the difference between helping someone out and later expecting a favor in return, or not expecting anything at all. People who demonstrate kindness toward others without expectations are considered magnanimous. In the Christian religion, this is called almsgiving, and in the Muslim religion it is considered the third pillar of Islamic doctrine. Understand, these actions are performed for others without any expectation or desire of reciprocity.

New behavior requires a change in thinking. As previously mentioned, in American society we are trained to expect from others something in return for our time or energy. Many Americans believe that "time is money," and therefore they think in terms of a "bottom-line" when performing service to others.

Yes, it is true, when we perform action, it requires work; work equals energy. It is energy consuming to help another. Yet, to look at this from a different angle, you are not taking the easy way out, you are doing a courtesy for someone else, so what if it takes some time or energy. Kind deeds never go unnoticed. There is a Biblical adage that says that you will reap what you sow. The literal translation could be the actions you perform now will be reflected in future events. In Eastern philosophy, there is something called karma. Karma is defined as the total accumulation of a person's conduct and actions throughout life, from this the final destiny of the person is determined in the afterlife.

A third element is *integrity*. It reflects the gentleman more than anything else. A gentleman must be a man of integrity; the gentleman believes that the truth does matter. It is his belief in honesty that delivers him from the contempt of others. He may not be correct, but he can be trusted. The reason for this conduct is based on the simple premise that a gentleman takes responsibility for his mistakes and accepts the consequences for his behavior. Because he strives to be genuine and sincere, lying or manipulating is not acceptable to him. The gentleman takes the high road over the low. He seeks to bring out the best in others. Therefore, people believe in him and respect who he is. This gives him confidence. One reason for this behavior is discipline. It is not an obligatory part of maturity. It must be taught. Discipline ensures that lessons are learned and that a price be paid if they are not. To modify a famous American military declaration, "discipline's legitimate object is more perfect people."

The gentleman's integrity is also reflected in his belief in knowing he is doing what is right. You must believe in yourself and follow what you feel is right. You don't have to conform to the crowd. It's okay to disagree with others. You don't have to follow anyone if you truthfully believe what you are doing is morally just. The truth requires you to be consistent with your intentions and not only when it suits your needs. Be confident and do the right thing. A gentleman has no need to impress others; his actions speak louder than words. A gentleman knows this and does not become obsessed by being validated. This is not affectation, but the way you really behave.

You should be honest with your intentions. For example, so many men are suspect immediately when they try to help women; it isn't the action, but the intention that is seen as fallacious. Why place others in a position to believe your sincerity if you have no intention of being honest? Most times, we get caught in our deception, which makes us impotent and thoughtless. Why put yourself in that position? Operate from the vantage of truth.

Being genuine doesn't imply weakness. Actually, it confers great strength. You will not be faulted for being honest. If you say something, have the backbone to accept responsibility for it. Be a man of your word. Tell the truth and be aware of what you say, and you will be remembered by others. People perceive this kind of persona as reliable. Manifest your integrity, be truthful. Remember, a gentleman thinks before he speaks and tries to temper truth with kindness.

Fourth, *reality is perception.* To others, you are not any stronger than your perceived abilities. Regardless who you think you are, other's perception of you is truly reality. Accordingly, a lifetime's worth of good reputation may be shattered in an instance if you misstep in front of others. As I have said above, our actions do speak louder than words, and that is what is remembered by others. Do not give anyone the reason to doubt who you are. A gentleman is aware that his reputation precedes him. A gentleman has honor. He also has a sense of humility. He understands that for every action there is a reaction. A gentleman realizes that dishonor not only affects him, but others. For example, if he is married, what he does matters to his own family, his wife and children. If he is single, it concerns his girlfriend or fiancé, and it always concerns his mother, father and siblings.

Fifth, and most influential, is *altruism.* Biologically, civility, politeness and etiquette are implements of control, both of self and others. Civility is one manifestation of control used by one human being to disarm fear or engage ego in another. Whatever the outcome, good or bad of this control, it is less important compared to the reasoning. As I have just stated, altruism or kindness is a noun describing the element I believe motivates people to help others.

As support of this belief, I invoke the thoughts of the fourteenth Dalai Lama, "Altruism is an essential component of those actions which lead to genuine happiness, we find that the spiritual actions we undertake which are motivated not by narrow self-interest but out of our concern for others actually benefit ourselves."

Altruism reflects a consciousness, an awareness of others significance beyond oneself. It is genuine and affords the practitioner gallantry or unquestionable grace.

Understand that the key to becoming a gentleman rests on having character. One expression of a person's character is demonstrated by the percepts I have just outlined. Having character takes courage and at times requires great personal sacrifice. For example, you must be true to what you believe while always knowing that your conviction may cause you personal harm. A gentleman must never be afraid to show decency or to stand alone.

It must be clear that our intentions are more important than our actions to understand our behavior. These intentions are shaped and molded by many factors: social mores, parental guidance, knowledge, economics and so on, and all are outside our control. Therefore, our character is capable of enriching or blighting those around us. Through observation, altruism, integrity, spiritual philanthropy and an understanding how perception is reality, we are able to manifest character that matters.

CHAPTER SEVEN

Being a Role Model

"Children aren't born with kindness; they aren't born to tell the truth. They have to be taught"

Michael E DeBakey, MD
Cardiovascular Surgeon

Do you know a gentleman you look up to, emulate or greatly respect? Like most men you probably have an idea of what you consider a role model, a mentor, coach or teacher whom you respect and admire. Perhaps you look up to a particular historical persona who had character, integrity or grace.

When I was a young man, Commander Neil Armstrong, America's most celebrated astronaut, was my role model. His accomplishment as man's first visitor to the moon inspired me. He motivated me to become something great. He demonstrated a self-effacing calm, as his candid grin and steadfast reflexes were grace to me. I wanted to become an astronaut and pursued a career in science to meet this goal. He was not only my role model, but my hero.

Try to answer this question. Whom can you identify as an influence on your behavior, positive or negative? Does anyone come to mind first? Most would consider a parent as the major encouraging and instrumental force in their lives. Often, issues of our character, belief, judgment and thought are directly related to their actions. This fact is something that follows us throughout our lives, at times inspiring and at times haunting.

Yet, just the mere superficial contact with some people has important influence also. Perhaps it was your uncle who took the time to help you learn how to cast your first fishing line. In doing so, it was not so much the act of throwing the pole or hooking your wrist that you remember, but the patience he had to teach you to do it after you had given up. Or maybe it was an English teacher who thought well of your high school creative writing project. His or her genuine interest became a catalyst not only for your career as a writer, but for expressing yourself. It might have been an elderly person, who seemed to know everything about life, and in sharing his experiences and thoughts you were able to understand something new about yourself.

Sometimes it doesn't necessarily need to be someone you have known personally. Perhaps it was a person you have never met, such as a legendary hero from the distant past or the present. Yet this person and the others like them may have had something in common, something unique or special. This person may have had a great ability to inspire. He or she helps to advance others in their aspirations to greatness, they become our role models.

Actually, anyone can inspire and influence not only just our behavior, but also our hopes, dreams, moods, and personality along with our core being.

As we continue to mature through life, people do influence the way we behave. Some people we invite and others we do not. This process is both active and passive. As children we act as sponges and soak up the habits and actions of those around us. The amount of behavioral influence is constant for children and adults. Adults just have less tolerance for influence due to a decrease in brain plasticity. Everyone has had a role model or behavioral icon at some point in life. For instance, what do Martin Luther King, Abe Lincoln, Jacque Costeau, Babe Ruth, and Nelson Mandela have in common?

Take a moment and try to answer some of these questions. Where do you draw your current behavior style? Can you define a quality or two that you might expect a gentleman to possess? Do you think it important for your relationships? Have you ever wondered why certain men are considered gentleman? Can you name a few people who have influenced you? Are there certain behaviors and attitudes that distinguish a man from a gentleman?

The men mentioned above are men who were and still are inspirations to other men and their innate style and personalities are unique and capture our imaginations. They were also men with a "common touch" and able to teach others important ideas. Some lead men to victory in their own way. Many people continue to look up and admire these men and draw upon their personalities for their own style.

Do you think this person had a particular skill or ability with which you identified? Or was it something else? Perhaps it was something not so visible. For example, perhaps you received a sense of integrity or honesty that made you feel that you were doing something *right*, that you were observing a higher standard. This sense of character is important for understanding why a gentleman is different from a average guy. It is character that separates them and their behavior.

Well known to behavioral scientists, people having a strong ability to communicate and to relate to others is essential for civilized behavior. It has been demonstrated that people who know how to do this have better job success, (it has been recently shown that these skills are more important than having high intelligence) and love relationships. It has become accepted that some people have characteristics and traits that give them an advantage in life. One popular study found that physically attractive people get more opportunities in life. If this is true, why wouldn't this be true for those who behave attractively? My experience is that people are aware of your behavior and it does seem to speak for who you really are. It can tell others where you are from, your level of education, how you feel toward women and your ability to fit in. Forgot the phrase, "clothes make the man," undeniably, your behavior should be the most important part of your wardrobe.

Whether the discipline is administered in the home, school or other institution, rules and codes of conduct are used to produce what is considered appropriate or expected behavior. What causes a change in behavior? The self-perceived expectation to perform for another is significant and in itself produces anxiety, and as we all know, fear of humiliation and disappointment are strong motivators. But what happens when behavior, social behavior in particular, is not expected nor reinforced? Nothing happens. The path of least resistance is taken and we follow the trends of the social majority, which may consist of peer groups, media and advertising or any other influential group. This social majority may be representative of the "norm," but may not strive for the ideal.

Therefore, it is a body of people that hold to ideals, traditions or behaviors, as found in the military, clergy or a particular group such as the Boy Scouts that inspires self-discipline and goals facilitating greater personal growth. It isn't just to be liked, but important for our health, as some psychiatrists and psychologists agree many of the destructive behaviors exhibited today are common to men who have lost their identity, sense of purpose and direction in society.

Do we need an ideal? Is there some standard that we must attempt to strive toward or is the weather vain of contemporary thinking all that is necessary to direct us?

At present, American men have many negative heroes, anti-role models and pop villains to draw character. The lack of positive role models in our present society has disabled American men. Many young men are no longer challenged to aspire to greatness, but are encouraged to achieve more superficial goals. There is nothing wrong with achieving material success or having status based on physical ability, but when emphasized at the expense of more important ideals, this pursuit debases men. In any case, striving for greater values and precepts is central to the cause of a gentleman.

Regardless of one's upbringing or intelligence, men must learn behavior from observing other men. American men need male role models who are interested in setting examples of good character. It is certain that some American male role models demonstrate exemplary conduct that inspires others, regardless of their worldly success. These men remember that their behavior will impact the lives of others, so should you.

CHAPTER EIGHT

How to be a Gentleman: A Gentleman's Code of Conduct

"A gentleman must acquire grace from all who seem to possess it, taking from each that part which shall most be worthy of praise"

The Book of the Courtier

As you are discovering, becoming a gentleman is no small task. Cultivated behavior and skills that prepare for the rigors of life are hard won. Just as any battle is won, you have to want it and aspire to improve yourself. You will make mistakes and you will fail at times, but you are evolving into something more refined by acquiring new skills and hopefully shedding some old habits as well.

You must adopt a philosophy. Acquiring a life philosophy isn't as difficult as it sounds. It requires living life with enthusiasm and sense of joy. A philosophy must drown out the noise of day to day living. To wake up day after day, work, and sleep is part of life, but it doesn't necessarily have to be mundane. Because Americans have directed so much attention on making money, our major life focus has become too narrow. To wake up each day embracing potential new experiences and opportunities is a chivalrous way of life.

The gentleman simply lives life, learning to experience everything, living life to the fullest by interacting, sharing and communicating with others. Living requires risk. It may present obstacles and often isn't fair and cannot be anticipated.

Sometimes we hear others say nice guys finish last. A gentleman never finishes last. He has confidence and self-control. A gentleman will inevitably succeed over all others. Most women love a gentleman and there isn't anything more they adore than a man who knows how to treat them nicely. But, you never know anything unless you really experience it. To do this, you have to know how to live.

A gentleman possesses a conscience, and he sensibly places others before himself. This is the most important axiom for the gentleman to live by. This he manifests by acquiring social awareness. The "me first" culture is based on selfish wants. A gentleman enjoys sharing.

He shares everything, a newspaper, a sandwich or his wife's kindness. He also enjoys giving, as the old truism says, "It is better to give than to receive." It feels good to give, to think of your fellow man and provide for his comfort and support. It is curious that almost every occupation is based on some form of service for others, a barber or a policeman, doctor or a builder, everyone does something for another.

A gentleman respects others. He understands that he may not have the same opinions that other's may have. He should caution against being hasty or reactionary when defending his personal beliefs. He is sensitive not to offend others whom he may not agree with or when he is confronted with ideas with which he has no experience. He must be open to other's thoughts.

Why condemn an idea or thought if you have just heard it? Respect confers strength of character and may apply to differences in religion, culture, gender, politics or any other idea. No one is an authority on truth. Everyone has his or her own interpretation and no one is absolutely right.

A gentleman acts as a leader, not a follower. He takes the initiative and is willing to lend a hand. He may not want to, but his intuition often leads him. He may live by the motto "hesitation is death," or he may slowly make his move. Setting an example for others through a simple, thoughtful action of humility by saying, "I'm sorry," is just as important as being courageous, both contribute positively. Again, the gentleman takes the high road over the low. He lets his heart direct his feelings, and in this connection, he knows what is right and what is wrong. He tries to bring out the best in others. If he can't say something nice, he doesn't say anything at all. To reiterate, the definition of a gentleman is not complex.

A gentleman is a man who places the concerns of others before his own.

He is a polite, gracious and considerate man who has learned, (key word: *learned*), standards of behavior. A gentleman is not born, he also does not innately have the skills that make him who he has the potential to be. He must acquire them. He must strive toward them. He is a work in progress, he is constantly evolving and may never be fully the man who he sets out to be.

Stated again, the gentleman manifests integrity. It reflects who he is. He must be a man of character. Integrity is essential to this trait. He must possess integrity. Integrity delivers him from contempt, he may not be right, but he cannot be considered deceitful. He may be trusted. He takes responsibility for his mistakes, and he will accept the consequences for his behavior.

Misleading or facetious thoughts and actions are not acceptable to him. The issues of "white lies" are just as any other lie. To lie implies overt manipulation and cunning, traits that are not considered good or worthy. To deceive only diminishes a gentleman's character. If nothings else, his character is his most sacred possession. He has self-control and self-respect, and these traits prevent him from advertising himself.

His confidence is derived from his belief in knowing he is doing what is ethically right. He has no need to impress others or gloat. He is aware his actions speak louder than words. Silently, a gentleman knows this and does not become obsessed with his validation by others. He is not bridled by insecurity and is aware that his reputation precedes him.

A gentleman has honor. He has a sense of humility, he understands that for every action there is a reaction. Regardless of his actions, they all truly matter.

To illustrate this point, the Alexandria of the modern age, New York City is a metropolis full of foreigners. This is most noticeable by observing cab drivers who have come from impoverished countries seeking a better life. In their capacity, they provide the raw man power that transports some of the cities inhabitants, some of whom are quite wealthy. As an observation over several years, many foreign cab drivers are naturally congenial and respectful. It is my remark that some of these fine men who, without wealth or great education, act more nobly than most people they shuttle about. Arrogance prevents a man from seeing others. A gentleman recognizes, acknowledges and respects all people regardless of race, creed or ethnicity.

Lastly a gentleman has sincerity. This is important because he feels that the way he lives is important to him. It is the difference between being a gentleman and acting like one. His actions are pure of heart and are not intended to produce short term gains or momentary impressions.

Derived from his philosophy and from those values described above a code of conduct may be developed which characterize the gentleman. A gentleman actually displays respect by being considerate to others. He displays deference to women and demonstrates this through his behavior.

There is an essence or quality to the way a gentleman behaves. To say again, a gentleman is no less a gentleman if he is not born of wealth. A gentleman may come from any social standing. He doesn't need an aristocratic upbringing or even a traditional family. He can be from any country and from any religion. His external environment isn't that important. His deeds are all that really matter.

The gentleman's code is a multi-step process requiring effort. A gentleman is never complete. He is constantly evolving, refining his character and is *a work in progress.*

Through observation, practice and experience the gentleman understands that nuance and subtlety makes life elegant and graceful. As to the acquisition of grace, one sixteenth century observer noted,

"And as the bee in the green meadows is ever wont (sic) to rob the flowers among the grass, so our gentleman must steal this grace from all who seem to possess it, taking from each that part which shall most be worthy of praise"

The Book of the Courtier

Remember, the illusion of physical appearance, clothing and level of education are less important to a man's character as is his checking account or fashion preference. The gentleman goes beyond this thinking. He adopts views and opinions that are considered truth, and perhaps, at times, his beliefs conflict with the status quo. He is a principled man. He will challenge what others consider more contemporary, more trendy or hip if it compromises his principles. Be aware, there will be many that will brand his style as too conservative, out-of-step, simple and dull, this is all right. The gentleman seeks truth.

He is comfortable with taking the criticism. Rest assured, the gentleman's behavior will be positively received by the majority. He must, however, accept that some will never understand, nor desire all that he may offer. There is little doubt that resides in the heart of the gentleman, because he is self-assured and confident, his actions represent his best intentions. Why are these chivalric behaviors fundamental for the gentleman?

They are important because they allow the gentleman to manage and resolve differences honorably. Just as reality is perception so is perception reality. Conflict is based on a difference of opinion, there of course are two points always present. How we resolve conflict says much about who we are, and our character. For instance, intensely contesting with someone is like arguing with cold wind, you cannot change the direction, or its bitter effect; it is wiser to create a warmer climate. Stop speaking and walk away. It works like a charm. In fairness, there are those who may result to violent and destructive behavior to solve disputes or arguments. Do not put yourself in the position to be harmed, always find a way out and live another day.

American society has been slow to accept what may be considered gentle-manliness. As this illustration points out, the social observer, Fanny Trollope in her book, *Domestic Manners of Americans*, provides a reason for the lack of chivalry in American male behavior and a reason for it to exist:

"Perhaps this unbought(sic) grace of life is not to be looked for where chivalry has never been. I certainly do not lament the decadence of knight errantry, not wish to exchange the protection of the laws for that of the doughtiest champion whoever set lance to rest; but I do, in truth, believe that this knightly sensitiveness of honorable feeling is the best antidote to the petty soul-degrading transactions of everyday life."

Being a gentleman requires having some awareness of tradition and an optimistic desire for some ideal.

CHAPTER NINE

The Gentleman and the Lady

"Women are looking for that special someone who is considerate not only to her, but to others"

Audrey M.

The chivalric character demonstrated may best be described by one nineteenth century English observer as, "The unbought grace of life, the cheap defence of nations, that chastity of honour, which feels a stain as a wound, which ennobles whatever it touches, and by which vice itself loses half its evil, by losing all its grossness"

Domestic Manners of Americans

We should strive to demonstrate chivalric behavior to everyone we meet. In my opinion, American men and women have forgotten to seek greatness in character. It is evident that many sex relations are based on exploitation. Men and women are unwilling to invest in one another and instead are seeking to know what makes each other vulnerable.

A more important sign of civilization may not be its wealth, technology, or grand buildings, but how women are treated by men. In other words, just how well men understand and appreciate women.

As men and women grapple with the complexity of balancing their families and their careers, the dynamics of civility are being strained as never before. As social attitudes change, behaviors once considered appropriate for one generation are no longer accepted or implemented.

For example, it was once customary for men to pursue women in the work place. This is a common place for men and

47

women to establish mutual personal relationships considering that the work place is where we spend a majority of the day. However, this environment has become increasingly hostile and work place romances appear unseemly. Notwithstanding real complaints of sexual harassment, men and women are more hesitant of socializing, and as sexual harassment lawsuits indicate, questionable accusations abound. The specter of sexual harassment has become a factor of life, and regardless of intentions, perception of ill-desired romantic intentions are reality.

The sociology of men and women do indeed tell us that we are able to accomplish more thorough civil courtship. Discussed before, due in part to sexual revolution, economic evolution, and the media culture, men and women have become adversaries. Both competing for wealth, men and women have lost their sensitivities and unique behaviors that were once the basis for a civilized romance.

Encouraged to compete with men early in life, women are developing predatory skills and are indirectly threatening men, and in turn men have collectively reneged women common courtesy and romance. Once customary, courtesy was expected from men when in the presence of women. Most likely, women have always been treated with courtesy and respect because of their special status as mothers or potential child bearers. Women did not object to this special treatment, and most still accept thoughtful and courteous behavior. The real difficulty is that men are now in direct economic competition with women and some men and women no longer feel that courteous and civil behavior is warranted.

Yet in regard to workplace romance, some men have subjected women to unreasonable demands, and some have physically and emotionally assaulted their coworkers and subordinates to assert control. As the majority of men are interested in just a potential romance, this current trend is reality and suggests men must be very careful and fear that an innocent attempt to court may be misinterpreted for something else. As a society, Americans are driven to produce, and our work life predominates our day, where is romance to thrive?

As a back lash to harassment threat, some men begrudge a woman her capacity to be both a mother and a colleague. This is unfortunate and offers to serve a stark example of a deeper social disregard for the American family and child rearing.

Can men adapt new behavior that is more conciliatory with the special requirements women deserve when they want to work and also have a family? Is competitive behavior between men and women really a source of resentment, or a component of something greater? One way to assess some of these questions is to look at some of the issues among American men and women.

It is up to men and women to effect change in their behavior. An American gentleman should advocate honor and respect for women and not harm their ability to maintain their feminine uniqueness. They should be aware that ill-conceived and imprudent behavior has consequences. The American gentleman should behave accordingly.

Moreover, a gentleman cannot live in a vacuum, he must have a lady to court. This means a woman must want to be courted and that they both possess the skills to do so. But let's face fact, are men and women really comfortable with courtship? Today, is it possible to court the liberated and educated women without offense? Do men know what is truly important to women? You may ask, how does this affect me? How does it affect my behavior, and does it matter?

All that can be said is that it is possible to court and the American gentleman is something different. He represents a new chapter in American male behavior and philosophy. By extending his hand, he wishes to have harmony and wants a peaceful settlement to the "battle of the sexes". The American gentleman chooses to understand women by not only appreciating their social achievements and economic desires, but also admiring and celebrating their femininity.

The future holds great political and economical triumphs as some foresee the twenty-first century dedicated to the woman. The American gentleman rejects popular boorish mentality by appreciating women for their abilities to achieve, to develop and to live their lives parallel with men, while at the same time understanding, appreciating and assisting in their unique ability to create and care for life. Yet, as this transition occurs, both sides have questions that must be resolved before victory can be savored.

First, some men are confused. What do women really want? Do they seek romance? Do they want a man to take the lead in romance? Unquestionably the evidence suggests that they do. Look at any movie, television show, or magazine, you will observe hundreds of indicators that male-directed courtship and romance are predominate female interests.

Now, what definition of courtship you live by is up to you. Courtship is confusing. From the European chivalric traditions, to American Puritanism, or the modern professional American woman's direct approach using coyness and moxie, there must be some compromise. For example, some young women are repeatedly victims of their own ambitions and often enter a paradox as they become quickly intimate with men without requiring an investment in time. They believe they will be pleased, but often their mutual experience results in unhappiness. Both should share responsibility for each others happiness. Regardless of morality, legality or social view, it is up to you to decide. All events have their place, and the timing depends on when you both feel comfortable. Yet, these issues are more confusing and are not easy to understand.

The term *moral relativism* explains the "standards" a society employs to describe what is socially and morally acceptable for others without regard to truth. There is real evidence that the moral relativism of twenty-first century American society is moving toward *biological realism*. Or the legitimate idea that men and women are different in some ways and the same in others, and because of these differences and similarities, should be allowed to freely express and accept them.

An American gentleman understands this philosophy and makes his decisions based on the respectful acceptance that a woman is uniquely different from him and courted appropriately.

To restate, the American gentleman is striving to demonstrate a more appreciative understanding of women. By celebrating womanhood, he remakes himself. He makes the decision to accept a woman's differences and admire their uniqueness. In doing so he satisfies a biologic commitment also. One not based on chauvinism, paternalism, oppression or fear, but from time-honored respect, consideration and kindness.

The American gentleman should understand he may change a woman's perception of himself if he chooses.

Feminism demanded equality for women, specifically, equal opportunity to an education and career choices; it allowed women to pursue economic parity with men. Despite the promise of equality, it was not intended to dispose of femininity, courtesy or even chivalric principles. Women still want a man to behave as a man, albeit civilized.

Men act inconsiderately because they are ignorant, insecure and confused. They are perplexed as to a woman's real needs. As mentioned, some men see the behavior of the modern women as counterintuitive. On one, hand women want a man who can care, protect and provide her a family, and yet on the other she presents herself as aloof and independent, perhaps even anti-feminine.

Some men do not know how to interpret the modern woman and are frustrated and perplexed. Their frustration can be separated into three parts:

- What does the modern woman really want from a man?
- How should romance and courtship be conveyed?
- Can chivalric courtship and romance occur without offending the modern woman's sensitivity?

Unfortunately, American men and women have few answers to first two questions and even with the best intentions, some people are not ready to honestly discuss the third. An American gentleman attempts to bridge these questions and offers his thoughtful concern.

CHAPTER TEN

The Lady

"We see that a word or laugh or act of kindness (however small it be) from a virtuous woman is more prized by everyone, than all the endearments and caresses of those who show their lack of shame so openly; and if they are not immodest, by their unseemly laughter, their loquacity, insolence and like scurrile manners, they give sign of being so"

Giuliano de Medici

One of the most difficult and most interesting demands of modern culture could be the determination of what we consider ideal. We are all exposed to the advertisements of products to make us thinner, smarter, more attractive, or less unattractive. We are bombarded by images that force us to judge ourselves against physical ideals.

Perhaps this is played out best in the American fashion industry. Ambitious, well-educated, financially secure and reproductively savvy, American women are leading, working and professionally succeeding to fulfill the American dream. American women have embraced fashion and due to their great opportunity to make choices, the technique for many is based on what is trendy or contemporary. Yet, why do woman choose to be stylish or conventional? Who do they seek to impress? Is there something more to all of this?

Over the last fifty years, social, economic, and reproductive changes between men and women have been extraordinary. Changing women forever, unprecedented economic gains have enabled a radical departure from more traditional roles of the wife and mother. Some American women enjoy the highest standard of living and economic affluence in the world. Highly-skilled, some American women no longer are reliant on men, enabling complete self-sufficiency. Professionally able, American women now achieve educational, financial, and political parity with men in most fields, and in corporate business they have made impressive gains and will continue this trend.

Yet, unfortunately, it is this direct competition with men that has generated the deepest social schism between men and women. More apparent in larger cities, young men and women face great obstacles today. Like warring tribes, men and women today treat one another as an enemy. Some play seductive games and attempt to subvert the other with cunning and deceit.

In as much, how would a gentleman describe an ideal woman that might interest him?

The description could begin with a subconscious characterization of any woman, his mother, relative or friend. Identifying elements of style and grace that are deeper than physical beauty, as the importance of her character will overshadow everything else. He might describe her as a modern, sophisticated or contemporary woman who also maintains traditional values.

She is able to not only appreciate her femininity, but also capable of forming her own opinions while resisting overt competitiveness. This woman of great will and capability balances her aptitude and skills with warmth and kindness. Always gracious, she is keenly aware of those around her and makes an effort to kindly extend herself, even if it is only with a smile. Her nature is to consciously accommodate others while maintaining her independence and dignity.

Elegance is noticed in her behavior. A gentleman may define a lady through her behavior, her style, or deportment. Her style is natural and displayed with confidence and sincerity. A woman of authenticity, she enjoys courtship and invites romance with the hope of maternity.

Above all, she accepts that she is distinctly different in thinking and being from a man, and cherishes her uniqueness. She realizes that to emulate a man's behavior would cheapen *his* distinctive qualities along with her own. She approaches life with a loving, caring nature that radiates to those around her with sense of excitement and wonder. She is able to accept gentlemen as unique and is moved by their different approach to life. This modern female is not competing for her place among men, but respectfully beside them.

As a single woman, her life is full of excitement and curiosity. Driven by passion for life, her mind is curious and she may seek knowledge and gather life experience. This modern woman enjoys travel and is open to experiencing new culture and people. She embraces diversity, filling her mind with images and ideas that will provide the social and cultural brush strokes for her eventual masterpiece, her future children.

This woman is not meek, nor is she an arriviste. This is a savvy woman with alluring charm fused with real moxie. She has the opportunity to be anything she chooses while knowing who she really is first, a woman.

If harmoniously married, the modern woman enjoys her home as well as her professional life. She makes her own decisions and also helps create financial stability. At a critical point, she may be willing to sacrifice her career and her social ambitions as a compromise with her spouse to provide her children a stable home. She is compelled to do what is best for her family. Also, she is in charge of her life and her children and honestly believes motherhood is her primary responsibility. As dean of the famous women's college, Barnard, Millicent McIntosh, a noted feminist has said that family life is the cornerstone of society and democracy. She as well believed the education of young women for motherhood was society's "most important task".

By no means will she slave for her man, but with team work, they both prepare their family to embrace life challenges. Triumphantly, her innate style of behavior reflects the compassion and tolerance needed for this duty. This woman does not fear tradition and embraces values that reflect her desire for her children's future. This woman also understands the role of being a mother and a wife.

Yet, as women vie for job parity with men and seek to compete head to head, some have forsaken their femininity, making their innate differences less apparent. Some have even abandoned their instinctual drives, as conception has evolved from a natural state to one that is somewhat contrived and artificial.

Modern America has set new standards in all aspects of life. The paradigm has shifted over a period of decades, as some American men and women have not just adopted non-traditional roles and behavior, but are creating new ones. Some women no longer are destined to work in the home, and are not expected to prepare the family meals, clean or care for the children as they now perform tasks that require years of education and advanced training, hours and hours of dedication to an organization. This has taken them away from the role of mother and has produced something different. Yes, working women have contributed to our enormously powerful economy and also to the loss of traditions that have help shape the behavior of their offspring. Out of necessity or choice, some women now remain home to perform household chores and family responsibilities. Are more women remaining home to rear children because they sense an innate maternal drive or are they just tired of the work place?

Some households are primarily financially supported by single women and to suggest that they reverse course is misguided, counterintuitive and detrimental. The point is to understand and appreciate these changes, while accepting the need to maintain traditional behavior that has biological and social importance. Often failing to appreciate each another's unique differences and subtleties, American men and women should honestly discuss these issues with one another and work together for our children. It is time for a renewed perspective viewing the interaction between men and women.

CHAPTER ELEVEN

The Gentleman's Conduct with a Woman

"If there is one feeling innate in the heart of man, surely it is pride in extending constant protection to a defenseless (sic) being throughout life"

Balzac, *Old Goriot*

Attempting to order a drink at a swank bar, Richard, a thirty something restaurateur was pleasantly surprised by what one woman enthusiastically said to her friend. As he sipped his glass of red wine, he noticed that they were having trouble getting the bartenders attention. Without asking, he nonchalantly signaled the bartender for them. The women thanked him for his concern and as he moved from the bar, he overheard one of the women say to her friend, "You know, I really don't know many gentlemen, but I think he was one."

As men and women try to understand one another and sort out what is necessary for good communication, some would say that what is really needed is just good, old-fashioned consideration and respect. As this example describes, Richard merely assisted two women, without depreciating them and without expecting something from them. Richard's actions were not significant, nor were they considered overt or patronizing, he knew that they could have easily attracted the bartender's attention.

Let's examine what distinguishes Richard from other men. How is he different? Simply, Richard demonstrated he could be a considerate and respectful man with women without trying to impress. As a gentleman, he acted decisively, with confidence and as he did not ask for their permission to help, nor did he expect to be thanked. Richard acted as a gentleman.

As stated before, too often the perception of a gentleman is fantasy. The physical gentleman is often fantasy, debonair and suave, we are to think of a man who is statuesque and handsome, clothed in finely tailored elegance. Comically, he is assumed to be financially well-off, smokes English cigarettes and drive a sports car. Terms like *bachelor*, *rake*, *dandy* or the *playboy* come to mind. Hardly, one does not have to act as James Bond to be a gentleman.

Being a gentleman is not an act. Quite the contrary, a gentleman is an act of being. Far from the illusion, being a gentleman requires work. Perhaps more work than most would like to think. Demonstrating self sacrifice and discipline, standing up for one's beliefs and ideals and fighting for what you think is right befall all gentlemen. It also requires thinking differently. Thinking from an entirely new and different perspective.

For instance, Jennifer, a forty-something mother walks with her stroller, along a crowded Manhattan avenue and observed a group of young men "cat calling" a well-proportioned young women. In her disgust, she approached one of the men and said, if that were your sister, how would you feel about your friends? He blankly stared at her and put his head down.

You see, Jennifer humanized the young woman, by linking her to someone he dearly respects, the woman became real, a person with feeling. All women are sisters or mothers of men.

Being a gentleman requires respect and action. There will be times when you will have to go out of your way for someone who may not for you. Other times your patience will be tested in spite of your good intentions. There even will be times you may receive ridicule for being nice. But remember, there is an essence or quality to the way a gentleman behaves, he is a principled man. He will challenge what others may consider more contemporary or fashionable behaviors if they compromise his principles. There is no doubt in the heart of the gentleman, because he is self-assured and confident his actions represent his best intentions. In life there are some that win and some that lose, a gentleman tries to play fair.

The taste of defeat is always bitter. If you try to engage a woman and receive the brush off, in the long run, and in the face of let down, never deny who you are. Yes it's true, there are many other fish in the sea and statistically, there are more women than men on the planet. An offense to pride hurts, but you'll have to just try again. Always walk away a winner. In the face of adversity or rejection, remember everyone has bad days, she may just have been laid off from her job or grieving over a recent breakup. Just give her space and be a gentleman. Never become disrespectful or dishonorable, no matter what happens. You have to be the gracious host at all times. Never be petty or spiteful, and never be anything, but a gentleman.

Specifically, the general behavior of a gentleman toward women may be best describes as subtle gallantry. Courage, boldness, determination and initiative are important, but a gentleman does not have to obsequiously throw his sports jacket onto the ground to help a woman over a puddle. Nor does he have to receive permission to open a door for her either. His attitude must be one of consideration, reflecting a genuine desire to provide assistance. Just assistance. To perform a service with the expectation of an accolade or even a "thank you" runs counter to his deportment. It really doesn't require much more than being respectful and kind.

General Conduct

General introductions. You should always do this with a smile and offer your hand. You should be willing to show a sense of warmth and sincerity on meeting this person. Yet, a simple, "Hi my name is John," isn't all there is. As you are introducing yourself, keep in mind their reaction to you, so that you gauge their receptiveness to you. Always try to remember a first name. One angle you could try is to associate it with someone you already know with the same name. The point of remembering a person's name is to demonstrate respect. People do enjoy hearing their name. There is no question that if you use their name they will respond to you more favorably. This leads us to when an introduction should occur. Try to introduce yourself to others near the beginning of a conversation. If you are speaking to someone much older than yourself, you should use a title. Mrs. Johnson or Mr. Smith, sir or madam, are acceptable and well taken especially if you both just meeting. Remember to look into their eyes when speaking. It feels nice.

Opening a door. A gentleman always holds a door for a woman. He defers to her, allowing her and any company she might be with to pass through first. By extending a hand for a few seconds, you should never let a door fall onto anyone after you have passed through. There is no exception. Revolving doors should be approached the same way. If the door is in motion, you should let her enter first. If it not moving, it is best that you enter first and begin the turn observing that her hand bag and clothing are not caught.

The elevator. Elevators have a mind of their own. For anyone caught off-guard between the closing doors know they can be a source of terror. The gentleman allows a woman to enter and exit the elevator first, always holding the door to prevent it from closing on her. When outside, you should extend a hand and press on the security baffle, just holding the open or close door indicator isn't enough. While standing inside, you should hold the door-open button until all are aboard. If it is crowded, a gentleman if possible, should disembark the elevator to afford easier ingress and egress for other riders.

Stairs. Stairs are a source of concern. It isn't only the clumsy or frail that get hurt. Even our presidents can fall and tear muscles. Remember that going down stairs is more dangerous than going up. It is this reason that a gentleman always precedes a woman when traveling down stairs. This is to protect her from unseen obstacles or to brake her fall if she should lose her balance. Many women do wear elevated shoes which do not provide ideal stability. When going up stairs a woman should not go first. You should allow her modesty and begin the assent first. This should be obvious, her modesty is at stake. No woman wants a man walking closely behind her, especially if he is a stranger.

Speaking with a woman. A conversation with a woman should be open to any discussion or idea, yet there is no place for foul language, name calling or yelling. Even though it is currently vogue to use expletives to give emphasis to, or punctuate what is being said. Foul language, swearing, cussing, profanity, it's all the same—entirely unacceptable. A gentleman should not curse. He should not swear, or use the Lord's name in vain. Common use of foul language is popular and seems to be completely acceptable part of American culture. It can be found almost anywhere. Why is substandard, unintelligent or vulgar language considered acceptable or the norm if a perceived majority practice it? However small, this lapse in civilized culture, it affects everyone and diminishes our ability to communicate effectively. It's just not the way to speak when trying to convey your thoughts to anyone. Although some men and women may think it is appropriate to use certain expletives, they end up appearing insecure and childish. A gentleman represents himself thoughtfully and respectfully.

The English language is full of colorful and dynamic words, try to use them.

Karen had just walked into a swank new bistro, when to her chagrin, she heard her name called from across the bar. Recognizing immediately whom the voice belonged she shot a scathing glance and then proceeded to join her colleague, Alberto, who was unaware of her humiliation.

This is a situation that is familiar to all of us. As humans, we do not like others to draw unexpected and unwelcomed attention to our presence. Alberto, in his enthusiasm made Karen feel self-conscious and uncomfortable. Whether across a room or large public space, regardless of the number of people, it is not necessary to shout and yell someone's name to attract his or her attention. Approaching the person quietly and identifying them with a nice smile and a polite, "Hi, I'm over here", is all that is required. Remember, offer an inconspicuous greeting, there is no need for others to be aware or disturbed by someone's arrival. Also, when attempting to signal a woman, it is a good idea never assume she will come to you. When practical, you should go to her, you want to make her comfortable and feel special. After you have approached, help her with her jacket or her baggage and remember to wait until you have reached within talking distance before you begin speaking, you do want her to hear you. You might find it polite to raise an arm to signal to her you have acknowledged her presence before approaching her.

If you are romantically meeting a woman, a soft kiss to her right cheek is appropriate. When conversing with a woman, look at her face when speaking or being spoken to. You should establish eye contact early. Avoid staring and overt glances that may make her self-conscious or uncomfortable. Staring at her bountiful cleavage or other revealing features is unnecessary. You may pay your respects, without becoming intoxicated.

Do not attract attention to yourself by talking in a loud voice or being overtly boisterous while laughing. A loud cackle is not a noise that others want to hear. Do not assume that because you're having fun others want to participate. If you are conducting business, it is a good habit to not speak about your competition in any manner that may be misconstrued as negative. Never use associates names either, you don't always know who is listening. Typically a man will act in this manner to draw attention to himself if he is with a particularly woman, please remember this is a sign of insecurity. If you chew gum, do so briefly after eating. Try not to chew gun during a conversation, watching a movie or at the dinner table. It just isn't socially considerate. Nothing is more unpleasant than listening to someone speak while they smack their lips. When you are finished with your gum, place it in a piece of paper first, this will prevent it from becoming part of some else's shoe.

Remember where you are. Before you cough or sneeze always place a hand to cover mouth, and always cover mouth when yawning. You constantly secret saliva and at times it may be ejected in a forceful stream that could potentially strike another person close by. It is a sign of respect and is civilized. Additionally, no one wants to see the inside of your mouth either. If you are ill or prone to a runny nose, carry and use a handkerchief or tissue. If you must pick your nose do so in the restroom, not at a dinner table or in the middle of a conversation.

Money. When you are with a woman you should always carry some cash. Cash is accepted everywhere and is the easiest way of making a transaction. Credit cards are fine, but there are many places that they are not honored. They also make a simple transaction cumbersome. Therefore, forty to sixty dollars is a fair amount of money and should always be on hand. More if you intend to be out on a date. Be prepared, you never know when you might need cash. When carrying cash, you should keep the bills neatly together. An elegant alternative to carrying money in a wallet is to make use of a money clip. Keep it in a pants pocket. Pickpockets usually can frisk a coat quickly and retrieve your money clip on crowded subways and buses. Never carry your bills as a heaped wad.

It has been said that Americans are consumed with money; making it and spending it. It was noticed even in the nineteenth century by a visiting Englishman: "He had never overheard Americans conversing without the word *dollar* being pronounced between them." Gentleman should refrain from discussing issues of money or wealth on a personal level in public. For example, if you observe a smart piece of jewelry being worn by a woman or a gold watch by a man, never ask her how much they have paid for it. Also, never ask a stranger their income. Money should not be talked of in public, limit this topic to the office or a private setting. Be considerate.

Using an umbrella. Invented almost three thousand years ago, the umbrella is a piece of human history used all over the world. It seems fitting that this is a device you should own and know how to use. If you are aware of the possibility of rain have an umbrella. Nothing is more elegant than holding an umbrella for a woman. There is something quite lovely about protecting a woman from the elements. After entering a building or restaurant from the rain, always remove your jacket upon entry. If you enter an elevator or crowded bar you may unintentionally soil the party you are standing next to. If there is a umbrella stand, use it. Place your umbrella in the umbrella stand when entering a restaurant or shop.

Posture. The way we walk or gesture is considered a form of body language. Your body movement and physical actions are part of the way you communicate with others. Often, more elegance is conveyed by being inconspicuous and not attracting attention to you. You may recall that impressions are made very quickly, usually before you speak a word. A gentleman's body movement reflects his level of self-confidence, his poise, indeed, his very status in life. The gentleman has polish. His is about confidence. Body alignment and proper carriage flatters clothing and prevents fatigue, thereby accentuating grace. Grace on a more practical side, provides a sense of unspoken consideration for others. For example, you must be aware that sudden movements may offend or frighten others, especially, in major cities, a gentleman should not move abruptly in close quarters as a little self-control goes along way. A suggestion is to not jump about, abruptly raise your hands or "high five" while in a crowd.

Body movement can also demonstrate something more, consideration. A sensual woman has a feline quality to her movement. So accommodate their natural grace and move accordingly. Be dignified. Be relaxed. Be yourself.

Escorting a woman. Walking with a woman, arm in arm is a form of physical and emotional expression, and a well-kept garden is not really necessary, nor is a lover, as you may enjoy a promenade with your sister or mother. You may ask, is it really necessary to escort a women while walking? Most likely at one time it was. To offer protection or sense of security, women were routinely escorted by men throughout history. Anthropologically, upright walking is a uniquely human activity. It also is dangerous, by exposing the most vulnerable part of our body, the chest and neck, we are not well protected from the elements or attack from predators. One way we have adapted to this form of transportation is to walk arm in arm. Although, modern men and women no longer fear attack by wild dogs or roving marauders, the reality of urban violence, wayward cars and pot holes are a concern. Therefore, escorting a woman is still important, whether it be formal or causal, professional, platonic or personal.

Now for the practical matters. On which side of his companion should a gentleman walk? How should he hold her arm? Should he lead, as in a dance? When should he disengage? First, a gentleman who escorts any woman be it, his wife, mother, daughter or lover should walk along the curb side of the sidewalk. This affords her protection from street debris and uneven surfaces. Think of the illustrative example of a man laying down his jacket over a puddle providing the woman protection. Today, cars whiz over puddles, splashing those who are carelessly not paying attention. Be aware of the road conditions. Guide her away from irregular sidewalk paving, uneven or unexpected surfaces. For instance, anyone who has ever walked over a subway ventilation grate knows how this could snare a heel or raise a skirt.

Second, you should allow her to engage your arm. As you begin walking remember to afford a space. Extend your upper arm slightly and bring your forearm perpendicularly into your chest. Allow your companion to insert her forearm, and then gently rest it on top of yours. The direction you are traveling will determine whether to use either use your left or right arm. Be sure to position yourself first and allow her the opportunity to engage your arm. Don't expect her to maintain the engagement at busy intersections, or when sidewalk or paths become too congested. Escorting a woman is like a dance. It's a matter of cadence and timing. Always maintain the direction and gently guide her. To lead means to think, and to plan ahead, but be flexible and remember to allow her space.

As for weather conditions, rain, snow, and the cold, all must be considerations. Have an umbrella, remove your top coat, (it is usually best if you take it off first and then ask her if she would like to wear your jacket), offer her what you have to make her comfortable. Living in a large city you may have to deal with the occasional panhandler. When solicited for funds, you should either provide a handful of stray coins or causally pass without confrontation.

Passing others on the sidewalk can also be a concern. It is customary to always pass another person toward your right, regardless of the direction you are traveling. Also, when observing mothers with strollers, little children or elderly always give them the courtesy to advance first, especially through narrow walkway and stairs.

Queuing. Standing-in-line has become necessary for almost every human social activity. Whether you are waiting for the movies, preparing to board an aircraft, or purchasing stamps you will have to stand in some form of a line. Therefore, you must be familiar with some of the perils of acting inconsiderately or arrogantly in an attempt to improve your position at the behest of others.

Mark was holding a spot in a long line for refreshments during a theater intermission, seeing that he was being held up by an group of elderly couples. Losing patience, he declared that he wished to also to make a purchase. One of the older chaps shot back that there still was plenty of concessions remaining.

Remember, you are not alone and there is no excuse for being disrespectful to others due to the mere fact that you may not ever see them again.

Do not step ahead of others in lines. There is nothing wrong with waiting, especially when you accompany a woman. The evening isn't going to be any more exciting if you rush your neighbor. Most will be offended and some will make a comment. Another way to create tension is to step in front of others to ask a question of a ticket agent or doorman without asking those in front of you if you may do so. Of course, if you are queuing up for preferred recognition at the latest night club be aware that courtesy is recognized on both sides of the velvet rope.

Beauty Peeks. David, a successful entertainment attorney was noticed by Jill, his girlfriend conspicuously purveying another woman at a chic downtown restaurant. Instead of being upset, Jill said to him, "You know if I looked like her perhaps I would attract your attention also." He sharply turned his eyes away and apologized for his gross disrespect. Later to her girl pal, Jill commented, "It was as if it was the first time David had ever thought about the way he treats women, and he made a wonderful discovery, me."

What David did was a cardinal sin; to look at another woman in the presence of the woman you are with is a faux pas has with consequences. Some may describe the reaction the instant pain of a scorpion sting or a python's silent asphyxiation. If confronted with the opportunity to observe another woman, remember whom you are with. Most women expect you to demonstrate respect and self-control, if you fail to do this in her presence, what is she to think when she's not around.

Undeniably, men are biologically designed to visually react to women, yet if someone does attract your attention, blatant staring must be avoided. Recognized by women as threatening behavior, to visually devour a woman's beauty is taboo regardless if you're single, dating or married. Many women state that this is one of the most offensive behaviors that they encounter. It is truly desperate and vulgar behavior. Additionally, men who give women the "up and down" may be immediately dismissed as a desperate fiend and usually are not given a second thought. If a woman appears inviting, and eye contact has been established, it is appropriate to slightly nod and smile, careful not to fixate on her for too long. Gallant subtlety is always preferred.

Display of public affection. Any display of public affection should have a sense of decorum. If you a prone to the impulse of passion and feel it necessary to engage in a deep kiss and embrace, remember who might witness your passion. If you are dining and there are other patrons present close by, be aware that they may not want to see your embrace. Be considerate to those who might be offended by this display. Children, parents, clergy and strangers all have feelings and sensitivities and may not appreciate this behavior. If you are alone or in a secluded area then you may choose to engage one another. Of course, we all have heard of airliner lovemaking and becoming a member of the "mile high club" may be thrilling. Just remember that you must be tactful and have respect for others. Public lovemaking is considered exhibitionism and can land you in jail.

Remember to have fun and think about whom you are with, try to go beyond the obvious and be creative.

CHAPTER TWELVE

Leading the Dance

"There is nothing more difficult to take in hand, more perilous to conduct, or more uncertain in its outcome, than to take the lead in introducing a new order of things"

Niccolo Machivelli

Over the last few decades, rituals of courtship have become ill-defined and capricious. Passed from one generation to the next, men and women once received instruction from family, friends and others that was consistent with a traditional view of courtship behavior. For example, men asked women out. They were expected to ask a woman to dinner, the movies or other social events and they were expected to pay. Based on the social attitudes of today, it is apparent that some women expect this courtesy and others shun it.

Yet, common sense dictates that men continue this tradition, as it is always an honor for a man to entertain a woman. How is a man to react to a woman's objection to tradition? On one hand he acts, based on ritual; on the other, he is confronted with an entirely different set of ideas. Traditional courting behaviors such as the act of asking for a date, phone calls, and first kisses are considered gender specific. As feminism has shaped social attitudes, actions once designated as solely male are practiced by some women today, as it is common for a women to ask a man out and pay for dinner. Confusing to both, who is right? How do men and women work out these differences while maintaining a sense of romance or seduction?

71

Men and women learn courtship behavior from their parents, family members, close friends and society. Yet, the primary learning environment is in the home. For many, the first experiences with romance are driven by the behavior of his or her parents. As the child becomes an adolescent he or she begins to assert personal behavior that will be checked by others. The acting out and the attention seeking of youth continues into adulthood. His or her behavior evolves into something unique in the pursuit of love. After a young man finds romance, he is captured from that point on and his behavior is based on seeking the feeling of love.

The Courtship Etiquette of the Gentleman

Courtship requires much more than you might think. There are some basic ideas you should know. Some general etiquette is required. There are no rules to acquiring etiquette really, just guidelines. Of course, some rules do apply to using utensils or that certain foods be eaten a particular way and you may want to familiarize yourself with them. But in reality there are only a few hard commands to behaving as a gentleman; you must learn through experience. You become familiar with certain behavior styles or suggestions and try to adapt your personality to them. You must be yourself. More importantly, you must be confident being yourself. Confidence is the single most seductive power a man possesses. Yet, do not come across as overly certain or you will offend others.

A gentleman should have a least a basic understanding of basic polite behavior. As stated in the previous chapter, knowing some basic concepts of general etiquette provides a framework for other forms of behavior.

Let us look at the art of the first meeting, the most magnificent and least primal of all interactions between men and women.

The Approach

The approach should always be respectful and dignified. The gentleman should make a lady feel comfortable, like she is being casually and discreetly admired. Remember, as a gentleman, you must pursue with a subtle air of indifference. Nothing is less seductive or less romantic than being too direct. Do not force yourself on her, be graceful and diplomatic. Although, take her curiosity by being sincere and tactful. This is where men get into trouble. They try to impress, show off and foolishly use a "line." Women easily sense insincerity and deceitfulness, just as the expressions states, "If they have heard it once, they have heard it a thousand times". Be honest, you may surprise yourself.

If you are waiting for her to signal you, or to provide you a sign, you might miss this opportunity. You should try to observe her body language and establish eye contact. It is this way you perceive her interest. Allow her to be comfortable with her surroundings, if you are at a bar or theater, you should allow her time to get comfortable, take off her jacket, find a seat or relax before you approach her. But, after making the determination to approach, do so. As you will understand, hesitation is death. She may be a minute from leaving, and you may never get another chance. If you are one who is indecisive, force yourself to have courage, and say to yourself, "I am a gentleman."

Introductions

One of the most important ways to begin any relationship is through a proper introduction. It gives both yourself and the other person an opportunity to engage in conversation and exchange information. As a gentleman you should always introduce yourself to a woman. Whether at a bar or restaurant, your cousin's wedding, or on an airliner, introducing yourself to a woman who has caught your eye is stressful. No matter how confident you are anxiety will exist. Brush it aside, this is just the nervous system being activated; your brain tells you that you must "fight or flight." In other words, you either take action or you walk away. Remember that fear is just a state of mind, and you are speaking to another human being, who just happens to be a woman. This is where some men say they wait to build up the confidence to speak. Remember confidence is your sword and shield and is highly attractive to women, use it carefully.

Now comes the easy part. Be yourself. Don't think, just be yourself. Go to her, smile, and ask her anything you like, tell her anything you want, just remember she is a person and be respectful and honest.

Conversation

To begin any new conversation, an introduction is very important, as in any contact with a stranger, within about five seconds, you will have made a lifelong impression. It is true, you never get a second chance to make a first impression."

You must make a good impression. This means having a firm grasp of what you want to say and delivering it with confidence. Confidence indicates to a woman many thoughts. She is able to appreciate that you are a man who knows what he wants, a man who is willing to take a risk, and potentially a man who may be willing to enter into a relationship. You may be thinking, "This is where I get off." There are no tricks written here, you may not want anything more than a good time. If this is the case you most likely will present yourself this way. Equally, the women that you meet may make fast work of you. Just remember the adage, "Like attracts like."

Most savvy women have heard it all. They will undoubtedly be able to spot disingenuous flattery. Do not fall into this trap.

If you willing to take risk, innocent flattery is very effective to break the ice. Drawing attention to physical traits is recommended as long as you are tasteful. Telling a woman that she has a beautiful smile or lovely eyes is a chivalrous compliment. The purpose is to create comfort and an opening to introduce yourself. Don't give her a reason to think you are less than who you are. Be honest and respectful. This will assuredly create a moment for you to introduce yourself and to begin a conversation.

Try to sense her desire for conversation through her eye contact and body language. If she is hesitant or appears uninterested, avoid being a boor. Just thank her for her time and graciously excuse yourself. No need to explain or apologize, just be nice and say goodbye. If she becomes irritated or rattled, you may want to offer apology for startling her, but you are human and don't take it personally. Just be open, honest and forthright. No lies, no stories to impress and no critical commentary. Be willing to speak your mind, but allow her to speak as well.

Always give her the opportunity to respond to you. Remember women are interested in discovering intelligence and some are not necessarily impressed by appearance. Their biological chemistry is different from a man's. They are not visually excited the same way men are. Science tells us that for women, it isn't so much about looks or appearance as much as mental ability.

As an aside, I have made a personal observation that who couples have real staying power are those that are the most physically related. Studies indicate that men and women get along the best and stay together, have remarkably similar facial characteristics and traits.

To restate, the most impressive and effective display of manhood any man can emote is confidence. Approach a woman with a smile; look her in the eye. Discover who she is and always be honest. Again be relaxed and be yourself. Let your mind feel comfortable being with her, anxiety is something you want to avoid, it shows weakness.

As mentioned in previous chapters, knowing how to politely behave is essential. Be nice. Don't curse, smile and speak. If there are other women around, act as if they don't exist. She will appreciate your interest. If you smoke or drink, do so with discretion. Do not allow yourself to become inebriated and uncoordinated. Don't be sloppy.

Your brain becomes somewhat stunned by alcohol and begins to allow dis-inhibition of thought and action. You will become loud and perhaps say something you might not normally. Remember that cigarettes act to enhance the effects of alcohol. They may also offend the women you're with or others around you. It is impolite to smoke and to speak to someone you have just met. Try to do what you can to afford her comfort. Be hospitable and inviting, show her who you really are, be a good man. Give her the courtesy to express herself with your full attention. Avoid interrupting her or going on about yourself, voice your genuine concern and appreciation for her company.

Again, the initial approach is based on confidence. Confidence cannot be stressed enough. Building confidence is not hard, if you think positively and believe in yourself. First, you must remember you are a man, and biologically programmed to take risk. Remember, irrational fear of rejection is just a state of mind. It isn't reality. Women expect you to approach them; do not expect her to approach you. They also want you to introduce yourself properly. For example, while at a bar, if you decide to send a woman a glass of wine and she acknowledges your gesture, go over to her. If you are waiting for a signal from her to approach, she already has. In fact she has given you two. She accepted your drink, and she thanked you for it. Now go over and introduce yourself. Be sincere and tactful, you may just surprise yourself. Women do bite, but you will survive, guaranteed. It really is easy when you understand women just want you to be respectful and courteous.

Observe her, take a unique moment to find out more about her, for example, determine if she has a significant other or is sending other men signals. Discussed later, body language and eye contact are excellent signals to observe and to recognize. After you properly introduce yourselves, begin the conversation, pay her a courtesy, compliment her, and give her your undivided and complete attention.

Setting the Stage

While in a conversation, it's best to think before you speak. Focus on her thoughts, key in on what she is saying. Your emotions can be hard to hide. You might feel the palpitation of your racing heart, sweat from your palms or a swell in your throat. This may cause you to say something awkwardly or to take time for you to construct a thought. Remember you have just begun a conversation and allow her to help you communicate. Listen to her.

Don't make excuses for mistakes in pronunciation, just keep it flowing. Slow down, breathe, speak clearly and find your voice. Have fun; this will allow you to enjoy her ideas and to loosen up. Refrain from dominating the conversation. Remember that you have put her on the defensive by engaging her, be considerate to her anxiety. Make her feel special. You are a man interested in who she really is, a woman.

When just starting out, it is best to avoid most controversial topics. Conventional wisdom suggests that issues of politics and religion may be best discussed after you have established a bond, but issues of past relationships or romances are potentially more damning. This doesn't mean you can't discuss these subjects. It's just that they really are not important at this point. You want to get to know each other. Be congenial, be pleasant and again, be yourself.

After your initial introduction and conversation, and you may find that you both have mutual interest. Propose a future rendezvous, you might suggest a coffee or a late afternoon drink, a walk in the park or a visit to a new exhibit. The idea that you might meet, and that it is informal and relaxed, again, removes tension. After agreeing to meet, offer her your card. Yes, have a card. Most reliable copy centers prepare and manufacture personal cards and are very affordable. Just be creative. If you have access to a home computer, do it yourself.

The card offers her three important pieces of information. It validates who you are and because your name is spelled she is able to visualize it and she will remember you. It should include your telephone number, with an answering service, and your email address which allows her to leave you a message if necessary. Second, it provides you elegance. No fumbling for a pencil and paper! No need to ask a bartender for his or her sacred pen. You are well-organized and aware that it is important that people know who you are. Last, you give her control. It affords her the choice of contacting you or not. You did not ask her for her number. You may think that women don't call men. This is the not true, they do. You can always ask her for her card or her telephone number. Let her have your card first.

The First Meeting

Consider the woman you met at the drugstore or on a plane does decide to take you up on your offer and contacts you indicating she would like to meet. You then wonder what to do next. Planning is the key. This is the secret to success.

It will make the moment by relaxing your apprehensions and let her know you are a organized man. Think about who she is, what she does for a living, what interests her, where *she* would like to go. Of course, when you call her you have thought about some places to meet and will have suggestions for her. Just try to keep in mind her interests.

Remember to defer to her; ask her what she enjoys, where she would like to go and have your suggestions ready so you may choose if she asks you to pick a place. Always be prepared.

If you live in a large metropolis or a small town, know the terrain, what the activities are, and if there is anything particularly interesting going on. Many major cities have guides that detail new restaurants and social activities. Don't be trendy. If you have a favorite hangout and it seems a good choice, go there. A comfortable and relaxed environment is ideal. Avoid the more difficult, less accessible venues. Also be creative with your planned activities. Taking her to a movie is not appropriate for you first planned encounter. You need to get to know one another. Sitting in a dark room for two hours is taxing and waiting impatiently for a table at a famous restaurant isn't exactly fun either. Keep it simple and easy. Be original and creative, an afternoon walk in the park or random window shopping can be exciting as well.

Remember, being with a woman is a privilege, not an opportunity. One way to show appreciation of a woman who has become an object of your affection is to give her a gift. A gentleman should show *consideration* by providing a simple gift, always allowing a woman to accept without obligation. Flowers are well received. Try to avoid the clichés: roses, especially red ones are unimaginative, white flowers, like irises and daisies are great, as they are aromatic and survive well next to her bed. Don't wait until you have an argument to send bouquets, they should be spontaneous and make a woman's day. Usually, it isn't customary for a gift after your first date, but it is my experience a nice bouquet is always appreciated anytime.

Meeting and Dinner

The wait. When waiting for a woman, it is important for a gentleman to always arrive fifteen to twenty minutes before your prearranged time. This allows you time to confirm reservations, adjust your clothing, use the restroom, prepare a spot at the bar, or anything else. If she is late, most women usually are as it is socially accepted; you are never angry, and will be overly generous when accepting her apology. A wait should be no less than an hour. Never leave unless you feel that you have made a real effort to accommodate her tardiness. With cellular technology, you need to have your phone with you. Leave word with the maitre d' or the bartender if you do decide to leave. Remember, you want to provide for her comfort, make sure if you are waiting for a reservation at an exclusive restaurant, and you find space at the bar retain an extra space for her, including a stool.

When she arrives, greet her with a warm hug and a slight kiss to her cheek. Help her with her personal possessions, make her comfortable; show action. Make sure to check her coat keep an eye on her to carry her bag or satchel. If there is only one seat, of course offer it to her, if she declines and decides to stand then you also stand. If there are no stools available provide her space at the bar, if there are men crowding the space, ask them nicely to make way. Avoid smoking at crowded bars, this is just a hazard for yourself and others. Do not smoke a cigar at the bar or table unless you have received permission from those around you. If she desires a cigarette, do not object or lecture her, just offer to light it for her.

After you have both settled in at the bar, order a drink. It is important when ordering you have some idea of her drink decision prior to signaling the bartender. Again, it is clumsy to hail the bartender and not be prepared. Understand he or she may be very busy, always order her drink first. It is common now to indicate the type of liquor brand desired, be it premium/expensive, call/pricey or house/cheap. But order what you can afford. If it is house liquor, you do not have to indicate brand. After receiving the drink, make sure you have placed a napkin under the base of the glass. This prevents condensation from gathering and then dribbling onto fine clothing. Make sure that a stirrer is in the glass.

Due to the mass consumption of alcohol by our society, I would like to say something about its personal and social affects. Alcohol, well known as a social lubricant, has formed the basis of many lively conversations and other social happenings; some might say New Years is not New Years without champagne. Whether you are just buzzed, wake up with a headache or go to sleep twirling into oblivion, there are consequences. Some are far more serious, alcohol may induce lapses in reason producing coma, death or destruction and over time it can insidiously turn the liver to stone. With the era of modern science, we just have begun to understand the biological affect it has on the living body. Wine, beer or liquor acts on the body or mind the same, regardless of taste or composition. By sedating and depressing higher brain activity, judgment, thought and action are impaired. Harmful to all organs, it acts to destroy the energy production of all cells. Functioning as a toxin, the liver and kidneys must breakdown and remove it from the body. With this said, it would seem very unlikely that American society would function without cocktail hour or keg parties. Yet, there are some important points that must be observed if one is to use alcohol.

It has become apparent that women are more susceptible to alcohol. Several researchers have discovered that alcohol is more easily absorbed in the stomach and is not broken down as quickly in women, thereby making women more prone to alcohol intoxication. Women are also more predisposed to chronic health concerns, such as breast cancer, heart disease, liver and pancreatic damage. There is no reason for a woman to be expected to "par drink" with men, and a gentleman should be aware that one drink for her may be just enough to impair her thinking.

As a side note, the famous "French paradox" of red wine and reduced coronary artery disease is really a constellation of behaviors that cause this benefit. First the French eat fresh food, lots of vegetables and consume smaller meals over longer periods of time. Second, they drink wine, primarily red wine with their meals; as this helps brake down fats in the gut and expedite digestion, in addition to an antioxidant effect. Third, they are likely to walk or *promenade* after a meal to help with digestion. Fourth, they love fresh garlic and eat loads of it. It is a very healthy herb, as a natural antimicrobial and the best cardiovascular guardian. All of these components help to assure good health. Bon appetite!

After you have had your meeting and after your drinks and have decided to part company, try to arrange for her safe departure. If you are using a cab, you might share the ride; make sure she arrives safely, and then travel to your destination. If you are driving, make sure you are both safe to drive; remember that driving under the influence is dangerous and is not wise. In most cities, it is easy to call a cab for transportation. Remember, save lives and buckle up.

Dining, The Entrance

A gentleman should allow a woman to precede him to the table or booth. It is nice to allow her to make an entrance first into the gallery, providing her a sense of attention and excitement. These are the things a man thinks about to accommodate a woman's need to show who she is, to demonstrate that she is appreciated. As described before, once arrived, a gentleman will assist her during seating. Perhaps help her with her chair or move the table to one side to allow her extra space. Make sure she has a view of the restaurant, or any other visual stimulating terrain. Once you have been seated, wait awhile to use the facilities, make this something you do while you're waiting for her. It is quite unpleasant for her sit alone.

After you are seated together, look over the wine list, determine what she might like and what you can afford. A red with meats and white with fish are all you need to know as far as wine in my opinion. After you have discussed with her what she prefers to eat, and it is a nice touch to order for her. Upon the waiter's inquiry you might say the following, "She'll have the escargot to begin and the grilled sea bass with mashed potatoes for her entree." Don't look like an arriviste by trying to order in French or saying precisely what is on the menu, just state it plainly and clearly. Most women would never object to this, although some might.

Table etiquette is something that varies with the situation; you may need to know how to serve from a platter or when to use a fish fork, but you may refer to other reference guides for this.

One note, all adults should know how to perform CPR, as more Americans dine-out now more than ever. Any Red Cross office will be able to assist you if you care to learn.

The occasional mouthful of gristle may be a problem. This is easily resolved by placing your napkin to your mouth, just as would to clean your mouth, but gently place the fat into the napkin then transfer it to your fingers. Then you may discard the fat to the floor of the restaurant under your table. Try not to place food into your mouth with your hands, even asparagus. It just isn't gracious and leaves your hand soiled. If you drop a piece of silverware, don't attempt to pick it up. Ask the waiter for a replacement. Never eat quickly, chew your food and never speak with your mouth full of food.

Dinner Conversation

Table conversation should be limited to topics that are not necessarily controversial or require great discussion. You are there to enjoy a meal and her company, not to vent your frustration or political concerns over a medium rare steak filet. This doesn't mean you treat her as a child—it is just not the place to create controversy or conflict. Ask her if she has seen any fascinating movies, or had any interesting travel experiences or new work opportunities. Engage her, enjoy her, and laugh. This is not serious business; this is what you work so hard for, the company of a woman.

To eat alone is one experience we all loathe. With this in mind, if the service is poor or the food is cold, make a note and voice your concern later with the manager. It is thoughtless to create a scene over an improperly cooked steak or cold spinach for the sake of having a perfect meal. If it is unbearable, of course, let the waiter know, but refrain from sending the entree back. Think of her and make the evening pleasant and smooth. For those who enjoy their mobile phone, please turn it off. Regardless of the economy and the Internet, business is conducted in the office, perhaps in the street and on the sidewalks, but not at the dinner table. You may rise if you like, after your date returns from the lavatory or comes in after you are seated, and stand until she takes her seat, it is a nice touch.

The concept of tipping demonstrates the level of recognition you have for another who is *working* for you. Service, or the tip, may be included or extraneous, and left to your discretion. The European service system includes anywhere between fifteen to twenty percent directly in the bill. This is nice because it saves you the time and energy deciding what to leave. Yet, you have no control over poor service. American restaurants or cafes are different. Typically fifteen to twenty percent of the subtotal, the amount before taxes, is adequate, more if the service has been personalized. Another rule of thumb is doubling the tax. It is not always necessary to tip a waiter who has been rude or pretentious or if service is unreasonably slow or a menu item is extremely poor and the waiter has been less than accommodating.

Never feel obliged to tip. Remember, it is your privilege not to tip. This is especially true if you feel slighted and have had a poor experience. However, never make a scene and refrain from complaining. Just pay your bill and enjoy. At the bar, it is customary to tip twenty percent or more if you know the bartender, otherwise as a rule a dollar a drink. If he or she serves food, treat the tip as you would with a waiter. It is usual and customary to tip anyone a few dollars that has provided you a special service including bus boys who are very quick to provide you special service or a hostess who has made sure to seat you promptly.

The Exit

After you have completed the meal and have settled the bill, you may ask her if she is ready to leave and you both may get up from your chairs. Again, allow her to walk ahead of you. If she has a jacket or coat, wait to help her with it after you have exited the main dining room. Once you are near the door and you have adequate room then you may help her with her jacket. If you have checked your jacket with a coat check person, remember to tip a dollar or two. Try to avoid using a toothpick in public, check yourself out in the bathroom.

Dessert

After you have had time to regroup, you may assess how the evening is going. By this time you are quite aware if there is any chemistry between you and your date. If you are having a good time, by all means continue to have fun. Part of the excitement is derived from the spontaneity of just letting feelings happen. A nice place to go might be a darkly lit restaurant or lounge for an after dinner drink and some light music. Often relaxing, they are easy on the eyes. The ambiance you decide may provide new energy and create a new mood. If you have been drinking, especially cocktails and wine, try to limit any other alcoholic drinks. A smooth cordial, perhaps a Drambuie or Cognac are nice to end a fine meal. Going to a local café for a dessert with coffee or ice cream is also fine.

Remember, order after you have both discussed the money. Let her decide. If she isn't interested, and you really are in the mood for a sweet, make sure you have two utensils delivered. She might reconsider. After finishing your after dinner drink or desert, a nice walk is great. A promenade around the neighborhood or park allows the evenings consumption to digest and lets you both enjoy some fresh air. If it is late, and you sense that she is getting tired, ask her if you can see her home. Don't wait until she yawns to suggest she go home. Be aware, observe her, sense her needs and act accordingly.

Also, remember you are her host. If she has intimated she is tired, appropriate a taxi or walk her to the car. If she has driven, ask her if she would like you to follow her home. Do not send her home on the subway. Pay for her taxi fare in advance or split the fare together. If you walk her home or ride with her in a taxi, once you have arrived, thank her for the evening and let her know you enjoyed her company. Give her the feeling that her presence was well-received and enjoyed.

After the evening, placing your hand over hers gives her the choice of reciprocating or relinquishing. Meaning she may move her hand on top of yours in solidarity of the gesture or may remove her hand easily. If she reciprocated, a soft kiss on the cheek will be fine. If there is real passion, a sensual kiss with a warm embrace may be enjoyed. Try not to overwhelm her; this is not the time to go full court. Most women will want this moment, but to create tension, to force her to wrestle with the question of inviting you home to further the excitement may send the wrong impression. We like romance and seduction. Women also like to feel that they are special. Always make her feel special. Don't give her the impression you are just interested in seeing how far the "evening" will go. Of course, we all want to have the sense of passion swelling in our chest. But relax, if feelings are going well, you will see her again. Spontaneous acts of passion may prove to dilute the magic. Romance is fun.

After you both get back on two feet, ask her is you may see her again. She will appreciate that you are asking permission from her for a future encounter. If you haven't acquired her personal number ask her for it. Discuss your schedule later, tell her you will call her and speak with her soon. Consider calling her if she has driven home to make sure she is safe. On the other hand, if your evening hasn't gone as you have envisioned and the vibes aren't strong, say goodbye and thank her for the evening. Don't be disappointed. Don't be frustrated, not everyone you will meet will match. Just have fun.

After you have completed the exit, be thoughtful and prepare for your departure. Being realistic and ending the evening graciously is your goal. Congratulations, you made her feel special and all the time you were a gentleman.

The act of initiating romance for a man is rooted in tradition. Putting on that dark blue sports jacket, wearing your favorite cologne, offering a flower bouquet and perhaps having light mood music in the background are nice touches to inspire romance. All this activity is meant to do one thing, set a mood. Developing romance is not based on one activity, but is the culmination of several, each with a specific purpose. The idea is to create a comfortable environment.

Arguing and complaining is the worst thing you can do. Be a man and be there for her. It works both ways. She may not want to go to do the things you want to do, but she may do it because it's about you, remember that.

Comfortable, non-threatening and familiar will set the mood and make her ripe for love. There are two words that come to mind when we think of romance. Sensuality and seduction. Sensuality allows you to feel and be felt, seduction is the art of pursuing these sensations.

You have to get into her mind; this is where the art comes into play. If you remember, during the initiation of a conversation one of the key points is to make yourself aware of the other person's receptiveness. Being able to do this is important because it provides you information so you may create a non-threatening and comfortable environment to introduce yourself. Create trust. This is the goal in romance, regardless if she is your wife or lover.

A woman is with you because she likes you. Please don't attempt to impress her by talking about the exploits of your past conquests, or how well you did in the stock market. Talking should be focused on exploring your immediate interests and what you feel passionate about. Forgot the blight of living, always be positive. Enjoy here and now with her.

Make her comfortable. Read cues, use body language and other nonverbal forms of communication to explore desire. Not having to ask, but responding to her unspoken requests allows both partners to appreciate subtlety and nuance, opening more opportunities for satisfying each other. Part of romance is also being able to back off, taking a nonverbal "no" for an answer, demonstrating respect for her. Again, create a non-threatening and comfortable environment; allow her to be herself.

Respect her by being aware of her feelings and acting appropriately. Taking responsibility for initiating romance is important, it should be shared, but don't allow yourself to forget her needs and desires after you have become involved.

CHAPTER THIRTEEN

The Gentleman's Biology Lesson

A joke. It was commented once that in Heaven the Frenchman is the lover, the Italian the cook, the German the engineer and the Brit the police. In Hell, these role are changed somewhat. The Frenchman is still the lover, the Italian is the engineer, the German the police, and the Brit is the cook.

The male brain is designed to isolate facts quickly and break them down to form quick, decisive assessments. As man makes these calculations he assigns labels, seeks to identify patterns, instantly determining a bottom line. There are many labels that men apply to each other. Some are harsher than others.

As with most male stereotypes, they cause us to think of different images, from a posture to the type of women they would attract. For example, the *nerd* is considered nebbish, weak willed and shy. The *geek* is a person who being socially inept often foolishly acts out because he seeks attention. The *boor* usually is defined as a rude, unrefined and tiresome. (It is said that a *boor* is a person who doesn't know when a conversation has ended.) The *slacker* shirks responsibility and skirts duty: historically, a man who evades military service during time of war. The *jock*, or male athlete, is considered a dolt, and slow on the uptake. Always portrayed popular with the women, the *rogue*, an unprincipled man, is a scoundrel.

We all want acceptance and we also want to belong to some group. Often, stereotypes emerge during post-adolescent life that can pigeonhole some men and are hurtful. Descriptive terms like nerd and geek, are common, but others may be equally as demeaning like jerk, slacker, or boor. What we are doing when we apply these names to men is reduce their character and injure their self-esteem. It is best to avoid assigning stereotypes or names to anyone. Remember being a gentleman is an art, not a caricature. You get the idea.

Speaking of the art of gentlemanly behavior, have you ever heard a women say, "Men don't know how to treat women" or "Men have no idea what romance means." These hasty generalizations come from valid observations that have been drawn from the basic way American men relate to women. The collective female opinion believes the average American male fails to meet the romantic expectations of average American female is not completely false.

Many women feel men no longer are capable of romance, considered by popular myth as: human behavior requiring thoughtful planning and execution of special physical activities designed to demonstrate emotional appreciation of one another. This is not the whole answer. Men need to do more than buy a bouquet and pay for dinner. They must be capable in demonstrating genuine appreciation for a woman. More about this aspect later.

Romance is based on a genuine interest that must be beyond just physical infatuation of another person. Of course, men have always venerated beautiful women and any heterosexual male will remember at least one spellbinding crush on a young *goddess* assiduously spurring flowers along with the mental preoccupation of her. Physical beauty is a catalyst for desire and may result in the pursuit of love's capture, but this should not be confused with love or even romance. Otherwise, infatuation is likely to mislead and confuse reality and be quite a shallow interaction, just as seduction manipulates feelings and creates detachment.

Physical adulation may contribute to romance, but alone cannot provide for the real emotions that are necessary for romance, such as respect, trust and consideration.

To expect romance to be practiced within a vacuum, or directed from one individual is foolhardy. As the saying goes, "It takes two to tango," it cannot occur as a one-sided activity. Plainly, romance is based on a gentleman's appreciation of a woman. He admires their unique differences, he understands they are biologically different, and that women are genetically programmed to want a secure mate who can eventually provide her a family.

Simply put, we cannot deny why we are here. We are sexual beings for a reason and both men and women serve separate and different roles in the attempt to preserve and continue their respective genetic codes. I emphasize, this is not to say a woman cannot perform roles that are not feminine, and that their only purpose or want is to become domesticated child bearers. It is important to appreciate that most women like being *women* and that they cherish this role. This is where romance lives.

If a man understands this concept, which is vital to understanding women, then he will be less likely to view women as one-dimensional sexual objects. He will think of a woman not only as a fellow human, but the daughter of a mother and father. Each women he meets he understands has the potential of being a mother also. Therefore, he treats a woman with respect and refrains from mentality that trivializes and diminishes her most important role and difference.

There are, of course many innate differences between women and men. It is not easy to provide a better explanation than seen in the phrase, "vive la difference." A gentleman is aware of a woman's feminine qualities and respects her as a thinking person who is capable of equal professional abilities and living pursuits. It is this appreciation combined with respect that facilitates and balances the gentleman's behavior without becoming paternalistic or chauvinistic. Also, appreciating their *otherness*, their femininity in contrast to male masculinity provides the platform for respectfully understanding a woman's differences.

For example, this may include a woman's ability to conceive, as well as her ability to nourish life. For example, the beauty to be aware and understand that her breast is a source of nutrients and security for human life. The way her eyes and the infant's eyes meet during the feeding is magnificent. It is important to appreciate the natural way she is able to provide and care for this life she created. A woman is the source for eternal happiness for a man, because she completes him, makes him whole. She is the flower in a field of weeds. Life would be miserable without her differences; physically, mentally and emotionally. This is what makes her a woman. Nothing should distract you from getting to know her.

One way is to first understand nonverbal indicators known as "body language." These behavior may be visually directed and be confirmatory of sexual interest and arousal. Scientific research indicates that more than fifty percent of communication is nonverbal. Body language or nonverbal kinetic behavior invite or dissuade others to understand our real feelings. To a person who appreciates nonverbal communication, there are many hidden truths that may be understood regardless of what is verbally said or not said.

Body language or nonverbal communication may be divided into several categories. The most primal form of man's communicative skills, personal space and posture offer information on situational security and comfort.

Just as fish swim together in schools and birds fly in flocks, humans also travel in groups. As number of like participants increases there is less chance of individual harm because the group has clustered itself from potential threats. This can also be a cause for alarm. There is a theory that when groups of people act together there is a greater likelihood that the members will do things they would not normally do. This usually is seen when men show off with their friends, willing to perform dangerous acts or "stunts" to impress others. The United States Navy "tail hook" debacle is only one vivid example this type of "wolfpack" mentality leading to a collective loss of honorable behavior.

More advanced forms of body language include eye contact and brow arching, oral display, head and neck movement, and body limb gestures. Each can indicate a level of sensual interest and sexual desire. Also, eye contact can provide clues that may reveal a persons level of interest. If provided in a positive manner, it offers its recipient the assurance he or she will gladly welcome an approach. Negatively displayed, one may not want to proceed. This obviously requires one to have a sense of the woman's potential gestures to predict a reaction. A woman may provide a series of distinct forms of eye contact or may combine several types.

There are six standard types of visual communication. The first being the most profound. The recipient of this gaze is usually not going to get very nice reception. The term, *gaze avoidance* is a cold and conscious form of body language that says, "Leave me alone, don't bother me." As an example, a man strolling through the aisle way at a grocery store may pass within a few feet of a woman and only to find her look through him, as if he did not exist. She consciously does not make eye contact by avoiding his eyes.

Gradually moving up the scale, a second form is termed a *one-second contact*. Positive in nature, a woman may observe a man and upon entering a ten foot proximity, may discreetly peer into his eyes, but quickly dart toward another object. Typically, she will not display this behavior in close proximity.

The next gaze includes the initial eye contact, but upon contact visually both male and female track together in a *mutual gaze*; usually occurring anywhere within five to fifteen feet, the contact results in a positive feeling for both. Even more intense is the gaze and associated *visual tracking coupled with a mutual change in physical body language.* A shift in rate of gait speed, turning of the head to continue tracking or brow arching indicates great interest and on exposure the heart often feels heavy and pulse rate quickens. Whether one engages the other is dependent on the male's confidence.

The most provocative eye contact stimulating pursuance and a strong indication of whether an approach is warranted is the *combination of the mutual gaze, body movement and a smile.* The smile has been documented throughout the world's cultures as a natural and spontaneous reaction indicating approval of another and friendship. All people exhibit some form of smiling when experiencing pleasure. Likewise, an approach would be very well received. As an effective and reliable type of nonverbal communication, eye contact provides a very quick and definitive signal of interest. There are other types of signals that may be slightly less conscious to indicate attraction.

Body movement and positioning establishes a more subtle line of communication when compared to direct eye contact, but provides the savvy man with a clear interpretation of her interest. A woman standing with one leg turned out toward the male may indicate strong interest, while a *back turn* will discourage approach. Other indications may be exhibited by *arm positioning*, arms held behind back or on the hips expose the breast indicating an unconscious sexual interest, but when crossed together over the chest reveal intense disinterest. Uncrossed or outstretched legs or hip swaying reveal strong to high interest, respectively. *Mirror movements*, as seen in "eye blinking rate synchronization" and "mutual head nodding" are a strong indication of interest during intense conversation. Arching of the neck, exposing the neck or slow side to side movement of the neck all are high interest markers. One has to be very careful not to over-read gratuitous behavior such as a "panty shot" or "waist bend", both of which are usually exhibitionistic behaviors and a sign of insecurity.

The most common and uncontrolled expression of interest is the act of *face revealing*. This usually occurs upon direct approach, and is demonstrated by the woman in one movement, the quick grasping with her index finger and thumb loose hair from her facial region and tucking the tuft behind an ear. This also occurs with unique eye contact. Prior to the tuck, the woman will look down or away, then after the tuck she will either look at the man or will look in a different direction, depending on confidence and ego. The tuck itself is a signal of interest, but a "post-tuck look" is a good indication that an introduction would be accepted.

Self-body touching provides the observer a reasonable clue to interest. A woman who slightly caresses her neck or arm during a conversation or other activity specifically focused toward a man, may signal a strong interest. While repetitively covering the mouth with a cupped hand or pulling fabric over an exposed chest is a concealing attempt indicating minimal interest. The exposing of inner wrist along with a light touch may be revealing. The subtle touching of the ear lobe or lip is a high interest marker also.

This entire nonverbal communication system is controlled by the brain and it is further directed by the autonomic nervous system. The brain, which is the center of thought and reason, also acts as the regulator of bodily function and control the body via the autonomic nervous system. The nerve conduit is the spinal cord and its nerve fibers and are distributed to the rest of the body. All information and ultimate control is provided to and dictated by the brain. To go one step further, the autonomic nervous system is further divided into two well-balanced control formats, the sympathetic and parasympathetic nervous systems.

(The most powerful format, the sympathetic nervous response influences how we react during times of stress.) Sympathetic control essentially attempts to preserve us from perceived death. It is structured to turn on during times of emergency. For instance, you may have heard of the "fight or flight" response. This means exactly that, we have two choices in most periods of physical threat to flee or to face the threat. That is why people will urinate themselves when faced with real danger; the body overacts by producing an intense sympathetic outburst. It tries to conserve blood by constricting blood vessels to nonessential areas, the limbs and genitals, effectively turning them off. For example, during times of intense stress, like fright, it is impossible for a man to achieve erection. The body disables the parasympathetic nervous system, thereby preventing the attitude for an erection or sex.

A penile or clitoral erection must be initiated by parasympathetic arousal before erection can occur. The nervous system controls the way we react, especially during periods of sensuality. If one is aware of the signs, it is possible to observe manifestations of the nervous system responses, and therefore possible to determine interest and desire. Visually confirmatory clues based on arousal can be seen by examining the skin.

One type of reaction involves, usually combined, and is "violaceus chest flushing" and "engorged nipple protrusion." The chest flush usually appears as a scarlet rash with a map-like configuration, noticeably at the center of the exposed chest in-between the collar bone. This occurs because of immediate and extreme dilation of the small blood vessels causing increased blood flow to the skin and sexual organs. Additionally, evidence of arousal may be evident over the top lip and at times on the tip of the nose. Known as "temperature unrelated sweat beading" it also is related to increased blood flow. The body is divided into systems, like a book with many chapters, each very different but when read together give a very distinct understanding. You may ask what causes these differences to occur? There are scientific studies that explain the hormonal and chemical differences between men and women. Personality and thought are intrinsically controlled by the impact of hormones on our brains. As our brains develop in the womb, levels of many different hormones in our mother's blood stream help shape its eventual function. Throughout life our personality and temperament is related to the endocrine glands that function interdependently with our body and brain.

Men and women have the same hormones but different levels due to our genetic sexual development. Yes, we are truly different. Essentially, male behavior is governed by testosterone, female behavior by estrogen. These are hormones that make us who we are. The ovaries of women also produce testosterone, but in very limited quantity, a small fraction of what men produce. Men produce estrogen in fatty tissue, again in very limited levels. These biological products produced within us make us able to reproduce. Hormones control the timing of reproduction as well as the moments of conception. For instance, most women's menstrual cycles are incredibly consistent. A healthy woman will ovulate roughly once a month from puberty, age thirteen, to their mid forties. The entire process produces the eggs that men will eventually fertilize to produce life; knowing a little biology makes it easier for a man to appreciate a woman's special difference. It truly is miraculous to marvel at her ability to conceive and nurture life. It is unreasonable to feel that a woman is just like us. It is equally unreasonable to demean their unique needs as well. Therefore, behavior is demonstrated differently and courtesy and consideration is deferential and preferential.

Displaying consideration demonstrates deferential behavior. Placing a woman's needs before yourself is natural. Her ability to continue life is more important than your survival. The stoic efforts of men on a sinking ship exemplify this action. Used before, the phrase, "women and children first" clearly makes this distinction. The reason for this thinking was to protect future posterity and to make sure that the group survived. This is gallantry at its best. This is the reason why a fireman or police officer will risk his own life to save the life a child. A gentleman is stoic and is able to shift his needs and wants to accommodate those of the common good. A gentleman realizes a woman is necessary for the survival of the community.

Preferential behavior is demonstrated with respect. A gentleman never shows a woman unflattering or offensive behavior.   He never consciously makes a woman feel uncomfortable or awkward. He never takes advantage of her sensibilities, and does not abuse the privilege of being in her presence. In other words, he makes sure that a woman has the compliment of knowing she is appreciated. He would never draw attention to aspects of her physical being that might be considered as critical or hurtful.

There is no conflict with contemporary female concerns of sexism with this thinking. Modern courtesy is not sexist. To provide women with preferential and deferential courtesy is opposite of discrimination against or devaluing women.   It allows the distancing of modern courtesy from less flexible traditional patriarchal control. For instance, it is not sexist to behave deferentially and preferentially because women receive kind consideration. In modern society, women are involved in activities that require them to behave as men. The have entered into professions and careers that require the same demands as men. For example, a female ophthalmologist and mother has to wake up in the middle of the night and perform surgery just as a man.

Yet, a male doctor working with this person in a clinic may be able to be respectful in affording his colleague preferential courtesy to care for her family. It does not ruin, but actually enhance honest relationships and strengthen society when respect and consideration is the focus; respect and deference both enhance the opportunity for open and honest communication. It provides a stable and predicable framework for courtship, and it is logical. It makes sense. Women, contrary to popular beliefs, enjoy and appreciate a man who acts with kindness.

Advantages of Being a Gentleman

You may be asking yourself, why should I want to become a gentleman? Strictly, from an economist's point of view, what advantage is there to changing my behavior and acting differently? To answer this question, it must be divided into two parts. First, how will it work for others; and second, how will it work for me?

Being a gentleman means more than being in control of the way you express yourself around others. Sure, having social skills are important, it helps facilitate efficient communication and make's people feel more comfortable around you. But as the world becomes more accessible and once distant cultures meet, we will eventually need an acceptable and standardized set of behaviors to interact. This requires understanding the differences and similarities between many types of people, and requires cultural appreciation.

Respect for others is essential for any successful social activity. There is less conflict and greater understanding of each other. Regardless if you are filling your car up at the gas station or having dinner with your business partners, respect for others shows that you acknowledge them, that they are accepted and have importance. As the core element to any good relationship, be it with a lover, friend or parent, promotes trust, harmonizing all participants. What could be more important to making life pleasant?

This in turn creates good will. There is the effect that the energy that you send out into the world is reflected back to you. This idea is a central precept for some of the major religions, Christianity, Islam, and Buddhism.

Being a gentleman requires exactly that, you are a gentleman under all circumstances. Consider for a moment what that means. If you need help, examine this illustration, suppose you sell real-estate for a living. This is a profession that requires real knowledge and integrity. You are selling the most important single piece of equity most people will ever own, perhaps even a life long dream for some. After a while, what you learn is that it isn't the information or knowledge that sells property, but your ability to gain trust. It is the same with being a gentleman. You must know some basic social skills, but it is the trust that you must establish that makes others feel comfortable. Remember that we have instincts. They are primitive, very powerful and invisible but, very real. We know when we are being deceived and we know when we aren't.

Trust also reduces stress and tension and helps promote a healthier society. It curbs sexual aggression and helps reduce anxiety, insecurity, and it improves self esteem, clearly one of the most important aspects of the way we define ourselves. Being trustworthy also helps establish a standard of recognized and acceptable behavior and eliminates confusion by creating behavioral consistency. These are a few advantages to changing personal behavior and behaving as a gentleman and how will it works for others.

To answer the question, how will it work for me or the individual? The gentleman himself benefits by becoming a role model, an important responsibility for those with a social conscious. It also allows him to express his maturation and abilities as a man not only to women, but especially to those aspiring to be gentleman, young men and children. Confidence, improved self-respect, self-control and self-esteem are all enhanced. How being a gentleman works for you could be summed up by an old American expression my father used to say: "You catch more flies with honey than vinegar."

Learning this concept usually begins early in life. History books are full of kings, caliphs, princes, and statesmen who, without caring supervision and the tutelage of others, would have not matured into the leaders they are known, such as Alexander the Great, King Philip and George Washington.

They all had received civil behavioral training early in life. Again this is the most important time because the period of just before puberty, pre-pubescence, human beings are conditioned to act or behave in accordance with those who are their immediate caretakers. As they progress into a more independent lifestyle they begin to acquire skills that are based on their own experience. During, these formative years of childhood, patterns of behavior are developed. The brain, designed as a sensory sponge, has the capacity to accept most sensory input, programming primal behavioral centers.

This brain area is known as the limbic system, and is responsible for our most intimate and essential needs. The drive to reproduce, eat, and fight is created from this finger-like neural appendage located at the base of the brain. All behavior is linked to the limbic center in some way. This primitive biological origin initiates the behavior needed to fulfill of basic urges, it also responds to stimuli that are equally as basic. For example, children are carefully reminded to behave through the actions of a stern parent or an even sterner teacher or principal imparting discipline, or a state of order based on punishment or submission. This is essential for establishing the immediate and corrective feedback for changing behavior and forming new behavior. This has been the premise behind corporal punishment and forms of shame and humiliation to form specific behavioral changes.

Those who maintain a commitment to establishing new behavior, some of which may be life saving, are often vilified for their unconventional and demeaning tactics that can prove disruptive and overwhelming to the uninitiated. A drill sergeant is an example that may come to mind. As the plasticity of the brain diminishes with age, the older a person becomes, there is more difficulty accepting behavioral change. The phrase, "you can't teach old dog new tricks," is partially truth.

The idea of being a gentleman isn't difficult to understand. It really doesn't matter who the other person is and it isn't important to try to read their minds. The essence of being a gentleman is just being nice. Kindness is universally accepted. There are few people in the world who do not enjoy being treated nicely. The more that you behave nicely the more you realize others will respond in a like-minded way.

They may not always return the favor, or treat you as nicely as you have treated them, but that isn't important. You cannot expect others to reciprocate courtesy or thank you for the way you behave. That just doesn't make sense. You are behaving nicely because you are nice, not because you are trying to get someone to do you a favor or expecting something in return. Moreover, possessing a sense of greater control over your behavior allows for one to develop the self, or super ego. In psychology, there is a hierarchy of developing self and is called "Maslow's pyramid of self-actualization". It is a measurement of attaining and knowing what is truly important for happiness. We meet the basic needs of food and shelter at the base and move through forming a sense of identity and relationships upward toward the top of the pyramid. At the apex rests the term "self-actualization", which implies that we are in touch with who we are and need nothing more than to be ourselves.

If we are aware of what we are trying to become, we can become that object. We can effectively communicate our need and develop skills to enhance what we enjoy doing. For instance, being considerate of others allows us to communicate more effectively because we learn by listening, we hear first and speak later.

Doing this with courtesy and consideration improves our reputation and perception of ourselves by others. This may prove more personally and professionally beneficial than we might imagine. Opportunities for positions of authority and leadership may become available. The relationships formed at work, with employees, coworker and employers will be better. The relationships between one's own family will also be improved. As mentioned before, romantic relationships will be improved and women will respond to you differently, especially when women notice the value of gentlemanly behavior and values.

CHAPTER FOURTEEN

A Gentleman and Sex

"Moderation in all things is the secret to a long life"

Anonymous

Sex must be viewed as the most important aspect of life. Otherwise, we would not exist. It must be clearly understood that the collective American viewpoint of sex is based on perversion. We like to keep it hidden and only like to accept sex as a curiosity. Incorporated into our media and marketing, the human form and most initimate purpose is reduced by exploitation and parody.

This perception will not change without a concerted effort to understand the physiology and purpose of sex. The nature of modern sexual relationships has moved from monogamy to polygamy. People have multiple sexual partners and are exposed to multiple microorganisms and viruses with the potential of serious illness.

Therefore, sexual considerations are not to be taken cavalierly, they present serious health concerns and should ideally be practiced in monogamous and caring relationships. Please give the following warning your full attention.

HIV/AIDS is currently a major cause of death among young people, childbearing age women, and children in the world. At the time of this writing, some regions of sub-Sahara Africa HIV/AIDS has infected one third of all young people. With no known cure, and few sexually protective behaviors to prevent transmission, HIV/AIDS poses civilization the greatest potential harm since the plague.

To reproduce is to live. The basis for this chapter was to lay a foundation for understanding the "scientific" sexuality of women.

After romance and establishing a stable relationship, a gentleman must know women and understand them. Part of knowing a woman involves reading between the lines, knowing visual cues, as stated in previous chapters, using body language and other nonverbal forms of communication to explore desire.

To reiterate, the mark of a gentleman resides in his ability to make others feel comfortable. It is a sort of general hospitality afforded to all he encounters. Deference, respect and consideration are the components of hospitality. A gentleman makes everyone feel comfortable and at ease.

As an example, when a woman has made a clear indication that she prefers not to engage in sex and her request is honored. Along with her verbalization, it is important to realize nonverbal body language can indicate more than what is actually being said. A gentleman must be willing to take the hint and back off. Additionally, when a woman says no, she means no. Always accept her decision.

It is a crime that young American men are expected to see women as sexual objects rather than sensual beings. The trend to package and market women has become common place in American media and entertainment and unfortunately shows the worst side of American society. Collectively, some social and economic groups have perverted the human form and sensual desire to satisfy American commercial ends. Therefore, it is incumbent upon men to be willing to accept that there will be times that passion will be initiated and that it should not necessarily imply sex. Keep in mind that she may be looking for affection, not sex when she asks you to hold her. Honor and respect her.

I have mentioned the difference between sensuality and seduction. Seduction is based on exploring her mind, exploring who she is first. The secret to seduction is conversation. The way in which you discover your partner should be from the inside out. The pleasure experienced by exploring a woman's mind is more than can be described in this book. Many women say that a man who can express himself with prose has a better chance than anyone else to fill her womb. The discoveries made during a penetrating and intelligent conversation lay the ground work for everything else.

During conversation, understand and respect her real desire, and then gage your attention and activity appropriately. The appreciation and respect displayed during this process can apply to all situations. If you are truly interested in a woman it is incumbent upon yourself to demonstrate this to her. Talking is not enough. You must show your interest. Be open with your intentions, don't hide feelings. Say what you feel, tell her.

Know the difference between romance, passion and lust. Physiologically, the difference between friendship, romance, passion and lust is based on the level of endorphin released and the period of time that it takes for the brain to become adjusted to the new levels. If a scale was created to demonstrate brain endorphin blood levels, the lowest end being zero and representing asexuality or low euphoria and the other end representing high euphoria or being in the throws of love. If you consider the level of endorphins released it could be said the more interest, the higher the level, and really is just a neuro-chemical event. Heroin addicts play this scale and live from one extreme to the other. If you have ever been in love, you know what it feels like to fall out of it. Despite the reassurances and the logic others provide, there is no question the feeling felt after love is dreadful. Acutely, you have a feeling of stomach sickness, you sense that your heart is sinking and there is a real heaviness to each beat. You are love sick, as you wear on, your suffering manifests a lack of appetite and insomnia. Your thoughts are consumed with the vain attempt to isolate a reason for your tragedy. As with time your memory begins to fade and the effect of this person no longer persists, but it still hurts.

The scenario described above has been described by heroin addicts as the same feeling they go through when they are experiencing opiate withdrawal, the event that occurs when they stop using heroin abruptly. This is a physiologic event based on the brains re-regulation from a high level of endorphin to a lower level. There are other neurotransmitters that are involved, but the main one is endorphin. To our knowledge, most of our happiness is based on this sole molecule connecting to specific receptors in the brain, and with its loss, most of all of our feelings of sadness.

For example, a romance can blossom unexpectedly with a friend or someone you may have known and had no interest in. It may produce passion and lust, but it seems that there are two events that may occur. Either you begin as friends, and a romance leads to problems, or that you are immediately moved from a friendship into love. The activities may randomly occur within the framework of this original event. Remember that many good friendships are upset by one night's passion.

It often is difficult to be completely honest with someone who has become part of your life. The reason for this is the simple fact that you do not want to hurt the other. You may endure emotional hurt, but you may not disclose the truth for the fear of causing the other pain. There is a saying that you must be cruel to be kind, which is at times what is necessary to effect positive change. It is not enough to dance around the subject and it only prolongs the agony to postpone the inevitable.

You will not be faulted if you are honest with the other, as long as you are tactful and considerate. Therefore, if you are not interested in her, then you must be a man and be kind enough to move on.

As said earlier, the biologic curves and hormonal flux of a woman are much more complicated than those that occur in a man. Any woman who is physically mature or ready to bear children will fluctuate on a monthly basis from the average age of twelve to the age of forty five. The phenomenon is called menstruation or having a "period." The actual bleeding phase is called *menses* and it consists of a normal monthly shedding of cellular material that has been prepared by the uterus, the upside down pear-shaped, hollow organ that acts a fetal incubator. In many primitive societies menses is considered an "unclean" activity and often the women are isolated from the men. This is patently false and no woman should be made to feel she is filthy due to this natural bodily activity.

Progesterone and estrogen are hormones that act in concert to prepare the female body to become pregnant. It is progesterone that specifically prepares the uterus for the ovum, or fertilized egg, if of course it has been meet by the male sperm. There are other hormones that prepare other organs for the future survival of the fetus, as prolactin and oxytocin are released by the brain to act on breast tissue. Lactation is the act of milk production and occurs if the breast and brain are in hormonal sync. The body is wonderfully designed as breast feeding women cannot become pregnant during nursing due to the effects of hormones.

Specifically, hormones are traveling messengers that traverse the blood stream to deliver precise and highly specific messages to organs. If you consider that women have about a third more hormones than men, men have very minute amount of estrogen and progesterone, then you may be inclined to believe that women may behave differently than men. Biologically, women are not designed to behave like men, nor are they physically or physiologically similar. For instance, science tells us that women on a whole are smaller, thinner boned, have less muscle, and enzymes and think differently than men.

They are capable of understanding and communicating differently, and they perceive or relate to instincts that may be more informative than any of our five senses.

Pay attention to her feelings; realize that a woman discriminates differently with whom she chooses to be with. The strategy is complicated, but women are attracted to men who have the ability to navigate people and acquire wealth. The more intelligent and verbally expressive, the more willing a woman is to establish a long-term relationship.

Most women are biologically programmed to seek out a mate who has the ability to provide for her future family.

This isn't to say women can't economically sustain themselves, it is just they want to develop a secure family. Women are interested in other qualities like appearance and youth, but they are not priorities like they are for men. Men are biologically hardwired to be drawn to facial symmetry and other characteristics of beauty. Women are typically more verbally articulate than men. They want to communicate and share there feelings, and they possess a natural ability to package and express thoughts that include their emotional experiences.

Being aware of this, it is often a woman whom men seek out for advice on emotional issues. A man would do well do realize women are not creatures of habit, but are constantly adapting and reacting to environment that help shape their behavior that otherwise might be routine. Women often do not get bored with things because they are constantly challenging themselves, they are programmed to. Remember, they are seeking a strong and secure mate to produce her offspring.

For instance, this is seen clearly in women who are able to move on from doomed relationships while her mate struggles to win her back. In nature, for everyone hundred males born, there are one hundred and four females, women are the stronger species genetically. If you question this, think about your own mother's accomplishment of giving birth to you. Women experience more pain than any man could ever conceive and are more able to adapt to climates and social instability than men.

Dismissing the mystical, women do have an uncanny sense of self and their relationship to others. Some women are more aware of their instincts, and this makes them very savvy. For example, some women may sense deception before you have deceived, then they may test you to flush it out. Often called a sixth sense or precognition, women in general are better at decision making than men.

For instance, it is usually a man who has to be reminded to use birth control when the need arises. Just a note about contraception, there is no behavior known as safe sex, just protected sex. Men and women should not have random sex, and if they do they should be very careful, and always use a condom. HIV/AIDS is very real and to date, deadly.

Women have much strength over men, but still want men who have defined character. Many women polled want a man who is genuine, honest and respectful. This is a common request. They seek a man who is honest and respectful over just wealth or status. This isn't to say she desires someone unemployed or poor, but a man who can support her and is willing to work hard for their future progeny. Do not ever underestimate the power of a woman or take her for granted. She may draw you from the brink and bathe you in her warmth or place you squarely in the ground.

Sexually Satisfying a Woman

As said before, the secret to performing any task correctly is well-thought out preparation. It surely holds true when pleasing a woman. The most important thing to remember is that she is ethereal, and like a precious flower should be treated gently. Her moods and emotions require delicacy and patient attentiveness, a woman should never be rushed or forced into any activity, especially a sexual one.

Second, you must understand her anatomy. Before you can fully explore you must have a basic understanding of where things are and how they work. Third, like any biological function, it is finite, a process that has a beginning and a end. The longer one takes the more fulfilling it becomes. Bear in mind that you are there to provide pleasure, not just to take it. You must provide reciprocity of feeling as well. Fourth, there are no rules. If you are both inclined to experiment than most of what you may try can be considered normal. There are some activities that may result in pain or tissue damage, and might be unnecessary, but still may be considered.

Basic anatomy. Differences and similarities between male and female anatomic structure are remarkably interesting. It should be understood that the primary sexual organ of the body is the brain. There is little doubt that the most fulfilling sexual encounters involve complete stimulation of the both the body and mind, as all sensory experience are directed to the brain for processing.

Mother Nature programmed males to become sexually excited by provocative visual imaginary. If you doubt this just look around, there are many examples of this fact being exploited. Sex sells and the reasons are obvious. Men are designed to quickly assess the reproductive ability of women. That is why features like hour glass curves appeal to men, they are the phenotypic signatures of a woman's ability to produce children. An hour glass physique implies two things. The most important, her hip shape and curve demonstrates her ability to conceive, carry, and deliver a fetus. And the second indicator are her breasts, as they signify her potential for the production of milk for infant survival.

Beyond these considerations, aspects like skin complexion may indicate that her system is disease free or that she takes care of herself. Skin color may indicate general health, for instance a very pale complexion may indicate anemia or one that is too dusky may herald liver disease. Men are attracted to women for many reasons. Intelligence, beauty, scent and body height all potentially excite men. Beauty has been described as "symmetry" and has been demonstrated in brain scans to cause an endorphin discharge when visualized. The brain is devoted to the visual system, which comprise the eyes and the connections between them and the brain. Forty-percent of the brain is required to process what we see. The male visual system is hard wired to the reproductive centers of the brain. Despite how hard men try to avoid looking at women, men cannot help visually observing a woman and to become excited. The question arises to whether or not he is able to discreetly do this as mentioned before.

Women on the other hand, are not as visually intrigued as men. Females do not have quite the same visceral reaction men do to women, but they do want a man who appears physically healthy. Many women are aware that men when given the chance will stray, and some think women may choose men who are visually plain, balding or older to discourage potential threats like other women. What attracts us to a person initially must not be confused with what keeps us together. Man is not designed to remain married for fifty years and die in his eighties. This is a recent phenomenon, only during the last one hundred years has the average age of male death moved above forty.

We are designed to mature and reproduce as quickly as possible. We must not be intoxicated with future time, the human body losses function every minute, which means we are in a constant state of dying. It is just recently, science has prolonged death.

When men speak of women sexually what do they really know? Where do they draw their information from, popular magazines, media programs or other men? Do you really understand the activities of a woman's sexual organs? Do you appreciate their physical differences and sensitivities? Do you know where they are located?

The five primary areas are: the breasts, vagina, uterus, ovaries, and brain. The breasts are large sebaceous, or oil glands that are tipped with erogenous erectile tissue, called the nipple, surrounded by the areola. This tissue is incredibly excitable and is linked to the central nervous system and the vagina by complex nerve relays. The breasts of women are larger, yet men and women both have excitable tissue and erectile tissue that form the nipple. As mentioned earlier, women's breasts are controlled by hormones during pregnancy, and when engorged and ready to lactate, fine, elongated muscular cells known as myoepitheial cells that line approximately sixteen ducts are triggered to contract at once, actually *ejaculating* milk from the breast ducts.

During stimulation of the breast tissue, it changes, as the nipple and surrounding tissue does engorge with blood and become firm. The nipples are linked by the nerve relays to the vagina and more specifically to the clitoris. The nipples and clitoris are the visible sexual organs that together, with the brain, when stimulated, produce orgasm. Orgasm may be produced by stimulation of either one, separately or combined. It is up to you to decide what you should stimulate and when, but knowing how to delicately stimulate this tissue is important.

The nipples are very delicate and highly excitable, they should not be bitten or twisted hard. A woman with a history of child birth may lactate if her breasts are regularly suckled and this is not to be confused with disease. The pressure exerted should be that applied to a grape before crushing it. Any greater pressure may cause pain, especially during heighten excitation. It is just fine to suckle them, but always be aware of the force you exert. Some women may have an increase in size of both their nipples and clitorises after child birth, along with changes in pigment as well.

The clitoris is well-hidden and should be gently teased into the open. It may be best accomplished by mildly exposing its exterior. The clitoris is a pea sized appendage that is located at the very top of the vagina and just above the urethra. The urethra is the opening that allows urine to escape. It should be noted that urine is not "dirty" and is not full of bacteria under normal circumstances. This tissue will grow, and can increase three times in size due to increased blood flow. There are the labia minora and majora that act as a hood and protect this delicate organ.

What exactly is erectile tissue? How does it work? As for the body's of men and women, there are more similarities than differences. You may ask how are the sex organs similar. While the obvious is that you can clearly see a man's while a woman's is a bit harder to distinguish. Yet, they are essentially the same in men and women, just different sizes and shapes

The erectile tissue that is part of the genitals comprise the *clitoris*, *labia majora* and *labia minora* and the *perineum*. In men these form the shaft and head of the penis, or the *glans*. Depending on whether the male had been circumcised, the foreskin is also excitable. With hundreds of thousands of nerve ending leading to the spinal cord and eventually directly to the brain, this tissue is truly the most sensitive in the male body.

The stimulation causes the tissue to swell and to be swollen with blood and life supporting oxygen. This causes a male's penis to become erect as well as a woman's clitoris. A woman does not demonstrate an "erection", but may actually develop a distinct enlargement of her clitoris that some in East Asian cultures consider a "third nipple".

The vaginal exterior or *vulva* is a term used to identify the entire exposed vagina, labia and clitoris. There are two labia, the outer labia majora and just inside are the labia minora, both are an inner fold of skin that work to protect the vagina from the outside world. The *vaginal labia* or lips contain glands that are sebaceous in nature. This is important to keep the labia moist and pliable from the constant exposure to the outer environment. The glands themselves secret very little oil. Just as the labia, the perineum is a fibrous band located between the vagina and anus and is highly excitable and can also become engorged. On entering the vaginal, or *introtus,* the front walls are seen a flesh colored and shiny. These are the *vaginal ruggae*, or folds and are constantly lathered in a watery-mucus film. This film is important because it contains healthy and needed bacteria that create lactic acid which defends the vagina from infection. It is a disturbance in this protective layer that results in an over growth of fungi, causing the bothersome yeast infection. Healthy women should not need to douche their vaginas as it is unhealthy and disturbs the natural environment. A wash with soapy water is all that is needed.

The walls of the inner vagina or *vaginal barrel* is about five inches long and is well supplied with tiny nerves and blood vessels. It is the intense supply of blood to these capillaries or blood vessels that cause copious lubrication, or *transudation* during intercourse. As blood is passed through the capillaries, the high pressure and high flow cause fluid from the blood stream to seep from the capillaries into the vaginal walls. Therefore, lubrication primarily is derived after a period of sustained excitement and may vary from woman to woman. This is essential to realize because many women suffer from painful intercourse or *dyspareunia* because they have not had adequate time for this lubrication to take place before penile insertion. It should be mentioned that some women who are may be *anorgasmic* are often just slow to lubricate.

The portion of the vagina that is attached to the uterus is called the *cervix*. As a circular ring it is about the size of a quarter and allows sperm to enter the uterus. It also has nerves that may transmit pleasure. This pleasure is different from the frictional pleasure that is felt from the vagina. It is here that deep penetration causes a woman to feel a sense of contentment and deep seated euphoria. The cervix is surrounded by glands that secret mucus, another minor component of her total secretions. This mucus is different from the mucus of the nose or mouth. It is usually thicker and more robust it has the ability to change over the course of a woman's cycle. During the premenstrual time, progesterone causes the mucus to thin, acting as a sponge to absorb sperm containing semen, capturing it for the uterus. A woman is much more prone to conception at this time. Additionally intriguing, there is a phenomenon that some women possess allowing them to produce a *female ejaculation.* Some gynecologists explain this event as a forceful release of fluid trapped within the cervical *fornices*, or recesses that surround the cervix during intense pleasure or perhaps from the uterus itself. Others believe it may be fluid trapped in the urethra and then released after intense orgasm.

The combination of the cervical mucus, the vaginal transudation and the labial oil secretion combines to form the lubrication necessary to overcome friction for pleasurable intercourse. Sexual arousal is principally the unconscious response to a combined mental and physical stimulus.

Paradoxically, sex is the most mentally and physiologically complex bodily function, even though it requires absolutely no formal training or experience. In other words, after we reach puberty, the body is preprogrammed to have sex. Being vulnerable and the threat of potential harm is something that must be overcome, and as you understand, this requires a level respect and consideration.

There are four distinct cycle's men and women go through that eventually lead each to orgasm. It is important to recognize these are arbitrary phases and may not be clearly separated from the entire act. Also, they may differ considerably between people and personal physical and mental situations. Women tend to require more excitement than their male counterpart.

First, during *excitement phase*, the body reacts to arousal by increasing muscle tone, causing blood vessels to constrict pooling blood in the erectile tissue, genitalia, breasts and skin. The initial response in females is vaginal lubrication. Due to the "vasocongestion", or swelling in the walls of the vagina, secretions form creating moist slick environment for intercourse. As this occurs, there is an expansion of the vagina walls, a thickening of the labia and an increase in the size of the clitoris. The nipples also become enlarged and may become erect and there may be an increase in the size of the breast. The physical changes may be slight to profound, depending on the women. Some women may have difficulty during this phase and it require extra time to become fully excited. Heart rate, breathing and will also increase along will the perception of the senses, especially the sense of smell, perhaps the most important sense during this time.

Second, after sexual activity has begun and during the *plateau phase* the vaginal walls may thicken to twice their original size. Filled with secretions, a distinctly musky scent that may be best described as pleasantly aromatic. The smell, scientifically, is produced by glands secreting oils that are broken down by healthy bacteria, creating musk. Different in every person, it should be considered an aphrodisiac and pleasantly sublime in good health. Some scientists believe that the natural scent that attracts us to one another is an immunologic indicator of compatibility.

The clitoris may become hidden by the vaginal labia, making it hard to see. Forming over the chest, back, buttocks and face, a "sex flush", or rash may develop in approximately half of women. Resembling a measles butterfly rash, it is completely harmless and indicates intense arousal.

The third phase, known as *orgasm* is triggered by an intense discharge of nerve impulses that occur after a threshold of physical stimulation, presumably friction of the clitoris has been reached. Women typically begin orgasm by simultaneous contractions of the vagina, anus and uterus. A complete orgasm requires a total body response, changes in heart beat, breathing and mental function. Women are different from men in that they may experience several orgasms and are capable of sustaining orgasm for longer periods of time. Multiple orgasms are possible for men also, they just require more energy. Known as "la petit mort" or *small death;* male orgasm can be challenging.

The final stage of the sexual cycle occurs following orgasm and is called the *resolution*. Women experience mental and physical changes that bring them to a pre-plateau state. This may set the stage for another performance, and more orgasm. Women are usually capable of several series of the cycle where men become refractory, or incapable of ejaculation for minutes to hours after orgasm.

What are the common sexual dysfunctions in females? *Orgasmic dysfunction* and *vaginismus* are the most common. Orgasmic dysfunction occurs when a woman has never achieved orgasm under any circumstances. Situational orgasmic dysfunction describes a woman who has attained orgasm in certain setting, but only under certain circumstances, for instance, as with self-masturbation. Vaginismus is the involuntary constriction or spasm of the muscles of the lower vagina. This can occur in response to a real or imagined attempt at insertion. It may occur in women of any age and may result in painful intercourse. *Frigidity* is a poor word to describe a woman who may reject sexual desire, and for unexplained or unknown reasons refuse sex.

The act of sexual communion or intercourse can be as simple or complex as you can conceive, it is all up to your ability and knowledge. Sexual acts like oral sex, termed *fellatio* and *cunnilingus* are the most intimate forms of sexual expression.

Going down or *giving head* are slang for fellatio. The method in which it is performed is dependant on the interaction of both partners. A gentleman who is aware that his companion may not be comfortable or experienced should provide delicate and respectful verbal instruction. By providing feedback you create an environment that is relaxing. Most women are aware that this is the most sensitive part of your body. They want to do it right. If you do not indicate your pleasure or discomfort they won't know if there are making you happy. Most women that have performed fellatio have developed a sense of your arousal, and when they realize orgasm is imminent they will either allow you to ejaculate or remove you from their mouth. Offer her either option.

Cunnilingus, or female oral sex, is the superlative way to prepare a woman for intercourse. The entire vaginal region, *cassolette* or "perfume box" is one massive nerve, and is only separated by the spinal column from the deepest recesses of the brain. A man who is accomplished in this art knows a woman very well and women adore a man who can pleasure her with subtleness and delicacy. A man should consider her actions and adjust his rhythm accordingly.

As the most beautiful act of human expression and communication, sexual intercourse is entirely a shared event. I will not offer any judgments, but being in love with your partner makes this experience truly meaningful. The physical act is unique and should be left to your imagination. Some historical authors provide descriptions based on positions of copulating animals, there are multiple variations like the *croupade* or rear-entry to almost any position a couple can envision. Reference manuals are available for those who want to know more about style. There is no reason for a man not to engage a woman in lovemaking during menses or pregnancy, as long as she is comfortable. It is truly the ultimate dance, and like any dance a man should take the lead, while always showing respect and appreciation for his partner.

Just a word on masturbation. Men and women masturbate to relieve sexual anxiety through the process of self-simulation and orgasm. Both ancient Taoist and Tantric teachings agree that semen is a man's most precious possession. It should not be carelessly wasted. Not so dissimilar to blood, and much more costly to produce; healthy semen contains vital nutrients, like amino acids, vitamins in purified form and proteins. It is potentially detrimental for a man to carelessly lose this fluid, as well as the living sperm it contains. Be aware, ejaculated sperm may live outside the body.

As stated before, creating drama in romance is something American men may not want. Many men withdraw from romance at precisely the time they should engage it. It must involve a man's active participation. Seduction is dramatic and dynamic. You have to physically show your emotions and feelings and communicate them. To do this effectively, you must be relaxed and make your partner feel comfortable. This is why a couple glasses of wine may be a nice way to break the ice, but maintain self-control. Sexual drama requires animation, real expression of emotion, laughing, smiling and eye contact.

Setting the mood requires more than lighting a candle or icing down the champagne, developing a sensual mood only requires interest and can occur in the middle of the night or during the day. Interest diffuses tension and allows for expression of love.

After a hard day, the best way to reduce environmental tension is to dim the lights, as it produces pupillary dilation, reduces, stimuli to the vision centers and quiets the brain. The senses of smell and hearing are thereby increased. The sounds of breathing, the scent from behind the ear together create delight. Enhancing the mood through sensual touch of the body's erogenous zones can bring each closer together while also preparing the body for the formerly described sexual cycles.

You should be a scholar, read and learn, understand how pleasure is derived. There are many steps and styles of the magnificent dance of intercourse. It is wise for a man to thoroughly please a woman before he is fully satisfied. It is never one sided, for a gentleman's pleasure is based on mutual affection. He is conscious of what his lady enjoys and makes sure that she reaches orgasm. Ideally this is orchestrated to occur together, as the mind is the most sensual and powerful organ. The connection between the genitalia and the brain is inseparable. The hard wiring of the female erogenous zones, the breasts, vagina and anus send nervous impulses to the brain and this is where the sense of euphoria occurs.

Allowing the primal man out, while using all your senses for exploration is one way to achieve pleasure. Part of love making requires discovery of the unknown. Don't be afraid to try things you have not. Read about sex, understand it is normal and healthy to try things that may be socially questionable for some, but always show care and respect. Sex play, dominate and submissive activities allows for role reversal, if you are curious and you both are up for it, try it. Just a word about anal sex. The rectum is a thin membranous chamber that exits the body through the anus, it is not designed for a penis. You must be aware and realize that serious injury can result if you are attempt penile-anal penetration.

Learning individual responses, anticipating your lover's wants and desires is essential. A gentleman applies his skills of observation to aid her pleasure. He anticipates her mood through reading body language and other nonverbal clues. He communicates. He shares with a woman what he thinks. This should happen both inside and outside the bedroom. Engage her thoughts before, during and after everything you attempt.

CHAPTER FIFTEEN

The Gentleman's Appearance

As our society becomes more affluent, men are becoming more interested in their physical appearance. Once a taboo subject, cosmetic surgery has become a real option for men who want to look their best, whether they want to turn back the clock or correct a natural imperfection. Also, the number of grooming products available for men are mind boggling. There are at least three medically prescribed treatments for balding alone. To help those who may be in the process of hanging onto what they have, most of the products do very little to deliver new hair. Save your money.

The gentleman's appearance is divided into two categories. First, is related to his overall physical well-being which encompasses his personal health and grooming habits. And second relating to the way he carries himself, termed countenance, deportment or carriage. First, last and always, you've got to be yourself.

To begin, a gentleman must care for his entire body. Hair, beard, nail and skin care are essential. Someone once said the true sign of a good lover are clean finger nails. A gentleman must maintain cleanliness above all else, and keep in mind that cleanliness is an aphrodisiac. A daily shower, weekly nail trimming, and monthly hair cut could be considered standard.

Daily bathing, with soaping and shampooing is the norm. With many men who exercise, you may want to shower twice a day. Inspect your feet and other areas for signs of athletes' foot; a fungus grows well in dark moist regions. It may present as blisters, deep cracks or fissures and lead to a red crusty rash. There are many over the counter medicines that eradicate it. Another region that may also be affected is the inner thighs and scrotum, the symptoms are usually a red rash and itching. Keep your anus clean, use medicated which hazel wipes if you are prone to sweating or hemorrhoids.

Acne develops during puberty and can last through the late twenties, due to the change in hormones and the level of stress that is experienced during this time. Acne is hereditary, and unfortunately, not easy to treat. Most remedies are folk lore and basically you must just out grow it. There are some men that are especially sensitive to iodine and bromide, and these are respectively found in products like salt and seafood. These may cause flare ups, so be aware. Food products that contain stimulants like caffeine and nicotine do as well.

Teas, colas, chocolate and coffee are the products with the highest concentration of caffeine. Found in plants, caffeine is a toxin that plants produce to protect themselves against predators, it is natural pesticide. According to their chemical nature, they are stimulants and these substances may cause higher levels of hormones to be released causing exacerbations. Topical medicines do little, but help to shrink the abscess. Solutions with an erythromycin or clindamycin antibiotic work best, but they really can't prevent it.

The best advice is to get plenty of rest, follow all exercise with a light shower, avoid stimulants and drink plenty of fluids, especially water. Our bodies are made of seventy percent water; we add to, detoxify and dilute our blood stream with water. Drinking six to eight, eight ounce glasses of water a day will improve the condition of your skin. It will also flush your system. Also, do not be afraid of seeing a dermatologist if you fear that your suffering from stubborn acne. It has potential to disfigure by scarring. It is important not to attempt to remove or express the contents of the abscess, due to potential scarring.

Think of the acne abscess as filled with "acid". The redness and tenderness of the abscess are due to the effects of the enzymes released by cells to destroy the bacteria within. If you squeeze of press on the abscess, the delicate walls that line it will break allowing these caustic enzymes to flow freely into other areas of skin. This will cause scarring. Try not to disturb it. You might apply warm moist heat to the area which allows this area to come to a head. This will expedite healing and recovery.

It is customary to brush your teeth daily and to floss at least three times a week. Your teeth are the most important part of your mouth. They will give you great pleasure or great pain. As for your physical appearance, your smile is as important as your hairline, perhaps more important. Do everything you can to take care of it. The typical American diet is rich in sugars and fats. Bacteria thrive off the sugar and fats that remain on teeth after eating. They cause plaque, a short of tart paste formed by colonies of bacteria along the gum line. These colonies form by-products, especially acid that erodes enamel and cause decay.

Brushing removes plaque and therefore renders the acids dilute and harmless. This must be done every day. Preferably twice daily, in the morning and in the evening. Using fluoride helps keep the bacteria in the cracks of the enamel to a minimum and prevents disease. Periodontal disease or other gum disease is caused by powerful bacteria that reside along the gum line. It is a major cause of gingivitis and root decay. Brushing at the gum line helps keep this decay to a minimum. See your dentist twice a year and get an X-ray every other year to inspect for tooth decay.

Also brushing helps eliminate bad breath. Bacteria that reside on and around the tongue are prone to cause this foul odor by breaking down fats and sugars. It is common is to scrape your tongue with a tongue scraper or even a butter knife to remove the bacterial coating that causes morning bad breath. If you notice a chronic problem with your breath it could mean other health concerns.

Basic grooming also means keeping hair tidy. Growing a beard of mustache is fine, it should be well-kept and presentable. There are many variations, like the Van Dyke, the goatee, and others that have a personality all their own. The way one wears their hair, such as keeping it long implies social statement, it may make the wrong impression. Rebellious and often requiring excessive time to maintain, it may be in style, but simplicity is what is needed. Occasional trimming of nose or ear hair depending on need is important too.

A wardrobe essentially should reflect your personality and style, a style that should be regarded as casually fashionable, but not trendy. Having a sense of clothing helps project an image. Knowing the difference between a cashmere wool and merino is interesting, but not important. There are hundreds of designers that supply men with their own sense of personal deportment and taste. Your wardrobe should be simple and comfortable; it should fit your build and personality. Well-known for the attention to detail and craftsmanship, French and Italian designers for men typically make the best clothing. Well-stitched, well-fitted and clean lines are the things to look for in clothes. It is always wiser to invest in moderately expensive clothes that will be worn regularly for years than buying clothing that will fade in style and quality quickly with time. Over coats and sports jackets are examples.

Shoes are more important than any other article of apparel you will wear. The rule of thumb should be two pairs of hand crafted shoes, one pair for casual and one for dress. A few well-known brands, Church's, Finistrier, and Bally are fine, hand-crafted shoes that easily cost several hundred dollars a pair. Figure one to three hundred dollars for a decent pair of shoes. This may seem like a lot, but shoes tell more about you than your suit, but be wise, don't spend money you don't have.

The most important concept to take a way is that you should be yourself and offer an appearance reflecting your education, personality and values.

CONCLUSION

"If ever our people become so sordid as to feel that all that counts is moneyed prosperity, ignoble well-being, effortless ease and comfort, then this nation shall perish, as it will deserve to perish, from the earth"

Theodore Roosevelt

The art of being a gentleman is a lifelong pursuit. I compare my motivation behind writing *The American Gentleman* to whatever inspires an artist to tease from cruel reality something beautiful. As my observations are of people, I have used their thoughts, behaviors and physical expressions to define character and grace while trying to outline the subtle essence of human behavior I find magnificent.

American popular culture and moral relativism are not the cause of American social disharmony, nor is the rampant materialism embraced by our nation, but rather the apathy and neglect toward improving ourselves as individuals. Some citizens of the United States of America live in a state of oblivion, consumed by an obsession for material things while neglecting what truly is most important; their community, family and children.

This misguided path is caused by many reasons and is beyond the scope of the book. Yet, the most important reason is simply the breakdown of the American family. Many American mothers and fathers are simply not *parenting* any longer. Many American men and women have become preoccupied with their own needs and have forgotten about others; consequently, they have dismissed their personal, parenting and social responsibilities.

It is this reason that commands American men to rethink their priorities and make necessary changes to become American gentlemen.

ABOUT THE AUTHOR

Michael James Hall, M.D., M.Sc. has written and published articles for various forums and magazines. His professional training is in the field of addiction medicine, internal medicine, ophthalmology, and he has expertise in health care management, law and policy. Dr. Hall received medical training from The New York Presbyterian Hospital - New York Weill Cornell Medical Center and management training from New York University. Over the years Dr. Hall has had the opportunity to live and to practice in New York City as well as, New Orleans. He currently lives in Kansas City, Missouri.

www.theamericangentleman.com

Printed in the United States
122527LV00001B/49/A